How to Succeed
No Matter What Life
Throws at You

RESILIENCE

AT WORK

Salvatore R. Maddi

and

Deborah M. Khoshaba

MJF BOOKS

NEW YORK

Published by MJF Books
Fine Communications
322 Eighth Avenue
New York, NY 10001

Resilience at Work
LC Control Number 2007939435
ISBN-13: 978-1-56731-902-6
ISBN-10: 1-56731-902-5

CONTENTS

PREFACE

We both started out as high-risk kids. Our parents were immigrants to the United States—they were economically poor and had little or no education. Our early lives were very hard and filled with challenges. Although our parents wanted the best for us, they did not know what that meant in American society or how to help us get it.

Fortunately, some of our teachers in the early years at school saw us as gifted and talented, and provided much-needed support and guidance within the educational process. We did not always get support from our schoolmates, however, as some of them saw us as smart, capable competitors. But, the support of our teachers helped us both decide to go to college, and to work at being successful there.

After college, Sal went right on to graduate school in clinical psychology, whereas Debbie concentrated on her singing career. Receiving his doctorate, Sal started his lifelong career as a college teacher, researcher, and practitioner. After some years as a singer, Debbie gave up this career and also went to graduate school in clinical psychology, received her doctorate, and embarked on a psychological career as a practitioner, teacher, and consultant.

Before long, the similarities in our career beliefs and efforts led our paths to cross. We both got into existential psychology, especially in how people can successfully navigate the turbulent waters of life change. We both locked on to *hardiness* as the key to resilience under stress, not only because our research and practice supports this view, but also because it fits with our own life experiences.

Now there is so much stressful turmoil in the world and workplace that we want to reach out to working adults by teaching the attitudes and skills we used to find personal and professional satisfaction and success. Hopefully, what we have to say in this book will help you turn stressful changes to your advantage.

SALVATORE R. MADDI AND DEBORAH M. KHOSHABA

RESILIENCE AT WORK

INTRODUCTION

As a people, we want to believe that we can learn, change, and master whatever comes our way. The ability to "pull ourselves up by our bootstraps" has long been one of our most treasured workplace traits. We have continually wanted to reinvent ourselves at the organizational and employee levels, which speaks to our long-standing ability to adapt to stressful changes.

What's different today? Contemporary social and economic pressures on an unusually massive scale make it harder for us to adapt in the highly developed ways we expect. Although we still want to believe in our ability to learn, change, and master stressful situations, today's tumultuous changes can be undermining, if we lack the capabilities that lead to resilience. Resilience under stress is more important than ever before. This book is about how to be resilient, to succeed no matter what life throws at you.

OUR STRESSFUL TIMES

The stress that we meet today comes from various sources. At work we are all subject to the ongoing stress of working with and for others. We may not agree on what about the work is most important and how to do it best, and we may differ in compatibility, values, beliefs, preferences, expectations, and working styles. This everyday stress can build up and undermine us. Add to this the disruptions brought about by global changes that influence our everyday living, and you have a recipe for high strain.

Perhaps the most powerful of the global changes are the breathtakingly rapid advances in telecommunication. Although the upside is the dramatically greater ability to accomplish things, the downside is the pressure to constantly learn more quickly, lest we be left behind in the "digital divide." For companies, this rapid technological advance has meant unexpected changes in goods, services, and markets. This has led companies to reorganize by downsizing or upsizing, centralizing or decentralizing, divesting or merging. This all has had major stressful effects on their employees.

Technological advances have fueled globalization. Although we can get things done around the world more quickly, technological pressures to streamline and homogenize operating standards and procedures threaten individuals' and even whole societies' traditions, values, and beliefs. We make decisions and plans with people we have never met. All these changes have disrupted our lives and made them more stressful and unpredictable.[1]

Ours are truly tumultuous times, in which spectacular social and technological changes multiply the usual work stress. It is all the more important today to do whatever we can to be resilient under stress, if we are to have a good life.

WHAT IS RESILIENCE?

When stress mounts, many people show strain-related performance and health symptoms. They worry more, feel hopeless, experience aches and pains, let problems preoccupy them, act like a victim, feel angry and bitter about the world, sleep poorly, and finish tasks inadequately or not on schedule. Over time, stressful symptoms can show up in wear-and-tear diseases, like arteriosclerosis, cancer, or obesity. These less resilient people show vulnerability under stress.

In contrast, it is resilience that leads us to thrive at work and at home. Some people are resilient even in extremely stressful circumstances. They turn disruptive changes and conflicts from potential disasters into growth opportunities. This is the heart of resilience. It's like finding the silver lining in the cloud. Resilient people resolve conflicts, turn disruptive changes into new directions, learn from this process, and become more successful and satisfied in the process. Take, for example, a manager who lost his job with his employer of twenty-five years, but used this as a springboard to starting his own lucrative consulting firm. Or, an employee who, rather than let her boss's stress-related outbursts undermine her work performance, eased his work pressures by helping him more. As our times become more turbulent, resilience has never been needed more.

HARDINESS AS THE KEY TO RESILIENCE

How can you be resilient under stress? You need to cultivate a group of attitudes and skills that help you to build on stressful circumstances, not be undermined by them. We call this pattern "hardiness." Hardiness emerged as the basis for resilience in our twelve-year, longitudinal study of employees at Illinois Bell Telephone (IBT), as the company and its parent, AT&T, experienced a catastrophic upheaval when telephone service went from being a federally regulated monopoly to being a competitive industry. In the massive, disruptive changes that ensued, the performance, conduct, and health of two-thirds of the employees in our sample fell apart. In contrast, the resilient third not only survived, but also thrived. They rose to the top of the heap, and felt more enthusiastic and capable, as they turned the changes into opportunities.

Compared with the others, the resilient group had the hardy attitudes of commitment, control, and challenge. These 3Cs gave them the courage and drive to face the disruptive changes. Through this courage and motivation, the resilient group was better able to

3

cope with the changes by finding solutions to the problems that arose and interacting supportively with those around them.

In the twenty years since the IBT project, more than four hundred studies around the world have further validated hardiness as the key to resilience. An important aspect of our research was to show that hardiness can be learned, by children and adults. Indeed, through this book, you will learn many hardiness-enhancing techniques, illustrated by relevant case studies.

OUR BACKGROUND AND PRACTICE

Our parents immigrated to the United States from other countries. Although they had big dreams and high aspirations, their immigrant status translated into economic hardship. This background classified our parents as disadvantaged and classified us as high-risk kids. Our parents saw their immigrant status as a possibility, rather than an obstacle, which helped us to adopt a powerful, resilient attitude. This and help from teachers and friends supported and guided our development.

After college, Sal went right on to graduate school in clinical psychology and embarked on his career as a college teacher, a psychologist, and a researcher. Debbie concentrated on her singing career, and after a few life twists and turns, she too started a lifelong career as a psychologist and teacher.

Before long, our similar career beliefs and interests led us to cross paths. We had become especially interested in how people can successfully navigate the turbulent waters of life. Both of us consult to companies and military and safety organizations, teach at the university level, and do relevant research. We locked on to hardiness as the key to being resilient under stress, not only because our research and practice supports this emphasis, but also because it fits with our own early life experiences.

We also founded the Hardiness Institute, a consulting and

training organization devoted to teaching people attitudes and skills that make them resilient under stress. The techniques and case studies in this book come from our years of consulting, assessing, and training at the Hardiness Institute. There is such stressful turmoil in today's workplace that we want to reach out to working adults and their families.

WHAT THIS BOOK WILL DO FOR YOU

This book provides you with techniques for building hardiness and improving your capacity to succeed despite stressful circumstances. It includes numerous examples and case studies drawn from our consulting work.

Chapters 1 through 4 explain resilience and how its underlying key is hardiness. By alerting you to the tumult of our times, chapter 1 clarifies resilience as thriving under stress and discusses key attitudes and skills that make this possible. Chapter 2 underscores certain personality features as important pathways to resilience. We do this by highlighting case studies from the Illinois Bell Telephone study. In chapter 3, we explain how key personality dispositions lead to resilient behavior. We also look at how the body responds to stressful circumstances. This is to help you understand how the body works and what it needs. The rest of chapter 3 summarizes the vast body of research on the performance and health-enhancing effects of hardiness. Chapter 4 makes clear that people can learn to be resilient in adulthood, and identifies the factors that help one learn to do this.

Then, chapters 5 through 10 present the nitty-gritty strategies you can use to be more resilient as stress mounts. Chapter 5 presents case studies that detail how and why the hardy attitudes of commitment, control, and challenge provide people with the courage and drive to strengthen resilience, no matter what life throws at them. We also explain how to tell if you possess resilient attitudes. Building on this, chapter 6 provides techniques for thinking about your experiences in a courageous way. Again, we use case studies to show how this works, and put you on your way to practicing resilience.

Chapter 7 helps you to understand more deeply how to cope with stressful circumstances.. Case studies are used to show the difference between coping efforts that are resilient and ones that are vulnerable. Chapter 8 shows you how to practice coping techniques that transform stressful circumstances from potential disasters into growth opportunities. Specifically, we guide you toward making stress more tolerable, understanding it more deeply, and planning and taking the decisive actions to solve the problems it creates. Again, case studies enrich your learning here.

Chapter 9 explains more deeply how work-based social interactions can advance or undermine resilience. We also show you the value of giving and receiving social assistance and encouragement during conflicts at work rather than letting these conflicts develop and persist. Case studies show you how to interact in ways that bolster your resilience. Chapter 10 provides techniques to successfully resolve conflicts with coworkers, bosses, and clients. You learn how to constructively assist and encourage others rather than to work against them and yourself. In chapter 10, case studies supplement the techniques.

In chapters 11 and 12, we summarize and extend the themes of the earlier chapters. Chapter 11 introduces you to ways in which resilient attitudes and skills strengthen your ties with fellow coworkers and with your employer. Chapter 12 explains how companies and organizations can build their resilience. We show you how organizations endorse values and create cultures that correspond to the resilient attitudes and resources of individuals. We further clarify how the climate and structure of resilient organizations supports their employees' coping and social-interaction patterns.

We enthusiastically impart to you what we have learned over the years about resilience at work. By immersing yourselves in the ideas of this book that follow, you can bolster your resiliency and reap benefits from these changing times.

CHAPTER 1

RESILIENCE IN THE
FACE OF CHANGE

*"A gem is not polished without rubbing, nor a
person perfected without trials."*

—CHINESE PROVERB[1]

As the twenty-first century begins, breathtakingly rapid rates of change challenge us to find new ways of functioning—as individuals, as members of society, and as employees. The way you handle these challenges goes a long way toward determining how successful you are in your life and your career.

Times have certainly changed, especially in the workplace. In the years following World War II, the United States enjoyed a period of relative stability and superiority in which the products and services offered by its companies dominated local and foreign markets. This led to larger, more secure American companies, expecting success and thriving on spirited yet relatively friendly competition, with their workforces assured of long-term employment and retirement benefits. In addition, most employees could look forward to annual raises and career advancement.

OUR TUMULTUOUS TIMES

The megatrends of change are everywhere today. We transitioned rapidly from an industrial to an information society. As time goes on, fewer and fewer jobs involve assembly lines and manufacturing. Because of the ongoing expansion of the Internet and computer technology, our work increasingly emphasizes the acquisition and dissemination of information and knowledge. But, no sooner do we learn a computer program or procedure than it becomes obsolete and is replaced by something new and better that we have to master. To keep up with this fast-moving, glamorous technology, we have to act quickly and keep learning. For all of its benefits, our high-tech world can seem to be a bit overwhelming, especially for older workers.

World trade and the communication it stimulates continue to spark an unprecedented globalization. Our work immerses us more deeply in a melting pot of lifestyles. The Internet connects us instantly to information from all corners of the world. We do more and more business with people we may never meet. Although this is quite stimulating, we increasingly encounter unfamiliar cultures, races, and religions that we may not really get the opportunity to understand. Moreover, worldwide, large-scale organizational changes redistribute wealth and increase economic competition and reactionary hatreds.

Organizational changes also preoccupy and distract many companies from adequately addressing employee and customer needs and effectively tracking essential marketplace developments. Old, established business patterns seem less and less effective today. Competition has become more cutthroat across all industries; companies unable to keep up fall by the wayside. To adjust and stay ahead of the pack, companies reorganize, upsize or downsize, centralize or decentralize, outsource, diversify or merge. Whether these changes decrease costs or bolster product lines and market presence to improve the bottom line, company reorganizations open a Pandora's box of employee problems. These include layoffs and the pervasive fear of layoffs, wage freezes or cuts, reduced hours, revised benefit plans, and hiring freezes. When there are no new hires, the employees who stay on must take on added work at no extra pay. To escape these realities, companies often make unwise business decisions to offset pressures on them. The ongoing business uncertainties affect employees everywhere; even the strongest companies have found themselves facing unexpected difficulties and been forced to change course.

Adding even more stress to today's workforce are the growing complexities of human resource issues. Although certainly justified, efforts to end workplace discrimination have led to an ongoing reconsideration of the criteria for hiring, promotion, and job allocation, making today's workplace a hotbed of social issues. Equal opportunity emphases impel employers and employees to make and implement unprejudiced workplace decisions and behave in accordance with these principles. In the short run, these positive advancements toward equal and fair policies can often complicate job assignments and promotions.

Change also can come in the form of new coworkers, some of whom may be less capable or perhaps less cooperative than others. Or you may suddenly find yourself with a new supervisor, a new department head, or even a new company president. Your current supervisor may start getting added pressure from above and, in turn, pass that down to you. Vendors and customers can cause new, unfamiliar problems that must be dealt with immediately, no matter how many other more pressing matters are piled up on your plate.

All of these changes, from the larger overall issues to the smaller day-to-day details, create stressful circumstances. It's how you handle these stresses—your resilience in the face of change—that determines whether you will succeed or fail.

THE DOWNSIDE OF CHANGE: EMPLOYEE WOES

Some of us choose to see only the drawbacks and disadvantages of the current work environment. For example:

■ Our job descriptions keep changing. No sooner do we learn some new technology than it becomes obsolete, and we must rush to learn something else.

■ The expanding digital divide alerts us to the peril that, though some of us will make it in the technological age, others will not.

■ Even if we have marketable capabilities, there is much less job security today than there was before.

■ Whether through merger or employment change, it is increasingly difficult to muster up loyalty toward employers who show little commitment to us.

■ We fear that family security and leisure are things of the past.

Admittedly, it is hard today to rely on what worked before and to know what will work in the future. It is tempting to escape taxing workplace pressures by denying or avoiding them. Alternatively, you can sink more and more into depression, self-pity, and hopelessness by worrying and obsessing over these types of pressures.

THE UPSIDE OF CHANGE: EMPLOYEE OPPORTUNITY

What is the upside of all this change? If you embrace change and use it creatively, you can open up opportunities to develop better ways of working and living. The key steps presented in this book show you how to develop resilient attitudes and skills for managing rapid workplace changes. By using them, you will turn stressful changes into golden opportunities.

Why do we react to change as a threat, despite its advantages? Because it is difficult to estimate how much a change will frustrate our wishes, needs, obligations, goals, and responsibilities. Such frustrations may result in losses, failures, and humiliations that seem too painful for us to accept.

To manage the perceived threat, you can deny stressful changes exist and thereby avoid them. But, you then risk losing valuable opportunities to utilize your brain's resources to learn and grow. To be resilient, you need to hold your fears of change at bay and capitalize on the opportunities that come with change.

WHAT WOULD HAPPEN IF YOUR LIFE NEVER CHANGED?

Similar to the evolution of the computer, the remarkable human brain evolved and grew in its ability to manage complex living requirements. The brain needs to function along its evolutionary design, namely, as a processor of new information.

If workplace disruption and unpredictability overwhelm you, you may prefer no change. Imagine your life without changes. Everything is predictable and nothing ever varies. This may sound great, but upon close inspection, a life with no change can be empty. Day after day, month after month, nothing changes, nothing new happens, everything is the same. Over time, the bliss of a predictable, unchanging routine gives way to boredom and emptiness. And, before long, you may look toward self-destructive activities, such as drug or alcohol abuse, just to shake up things. If this happens, you forgo many chances to advance your life in satisfying, purposeful, and meaningful ways.

Novel, changing stimuli make best use of the brain's resources that otherwise lie dormant. You can sink into boredom, apathy, meaninglessness, depression, and incapability with insufficient sensory input. The saying "use it or lose it" applies here.

THE POWER OF RESILIENCE

As stresses mount, many people become undermined in their performance, conduct, or health. They may fail to meet deadlines or reach goals. They may cut corners and disregard rules. They may have sleep problems, headaches, upset stomachs, or even worse symptoms as the time spent under stress increases.

Experiencing the same stressful circumstances, however, some people will be resilient, and survive rather than be undermined. Their performance, conduct, and health will remain unaffected, as they find ways to shoulder all the different kinds of stress. Further, some of these resilient people will not only survive, but actually thrive. They will thrive by finding ways to turn stressful circumstances into opportunities for personal growth. So, they will actually be better off than they were before.

For example, suppose that job insecurity is the source of an employee's stress, as information mounts that the company will be downsizing. The resilient employees who survive will continue to work effectively, and stay within the rules, despite the anxious uncertainty. And, those among them who not only survive, but also thrive, will struggle to discover what they can do under the circumstances that will make them more valuable to the company, and take the necessary steps leading to that goal. In this process, they will likely feel vibrant rather than symptomatic.

Lou Zamperini is a good example of resiliency. He not only survived great, even life-threatening stress, he managed to thrive in spite of it.[2] Through athletics, he learned to strive competitively to attain goals. His stellar high school and college performance as a sprinter eventually won him a spot on the U.S. Olympic team in 1936. Then, World War II broke out, and Lou began missions with the U.S. Air Force. While on a bombing run over enemy territory, his plane was shot down. Although he survived, he became a prisoner of war. Enemy forces tortured Lou to get him to reveal classified information. He withstood this assault and eventually escaped.

Upon returning to Allied forces, Lou restarted bombing missions for the U.S. Air Force. For a second time, his plane went down in the Pacific Ocean, but this time it was due to mechanical malfunction. He and his crew faced life-threatening challenges. Lou stayed strong and helped crew members survive in severe weather conditions and without food while awaiting rescue.

Fortunately, U.S. forces rescued them, and Lou returned to active war duty. When the war ended, he returned to the United States to start his business career. The same resilience that led him to survive and thrive in the challenges of war helped him to become a successful corporate executive. Although retired today, Lou Zamperini lives an active, vibrant life.

THE KEY TO RESILIENCE IS HARDINESS

Lou Zamperini has a hardiness ingrained in his personality that helps him and others like him cope resiliently with stressful life changes. This hardiness enables them to courageously face potentially disruptive changes and turn adversity into advantageous opportunity.

As you will see throughout this book, hardiness is a particular pattern of attitudes and skills that helps you to be resilient by surviving and thriving under stress. The attitudes are the 3Cs of commitment, control, and challenge. If you are strong in the 3Cs, you believe that, as times get tough, it is best for you to stay involved with the people and events around you (commitment) rather than to pull out, to keep trying to influence the outcomes in which you are involved (control) rather than to give up, and to try to discover how you and others can grow through the stress (challenge) rather than to bemoan your fate. These 3Cs amount to the courage and motivation to do the hard but important work of using stressful circumstances to your advantage.

Success in the hard work just mentioned involves using the

skills of coping to solve problems and interacting with others to deepen social support. In transformational coping, you first take the mental steps of broadening your perspective on and deepening your understanding of the stressful circumstance. Building on this, you then plan and carry out a decisive course of action to resolve the stress. In interacting with the people around you, you give and receive assistance and encouragement, deepening social support so conflicts can be resolved. It is the combination of hardy attitudes and skills that helps people survive and thrive under stress. Luckily, resilience is not just an ability one is born with, but something anyone can learn and improve. With more than twenty years of hardiness research and practice, we have shown that, if you want to thrive in the twenty-first century, you need to have internal hardiness resources to manage workplace stress. Now we want to pass on to you what we have learned—to help you develop resilience at work.

CHAPTER 2

RESEARCHING STRESS AND RESILIENCY

In the 1970s, social science research on stress became fodder for human-potential movements that warned of its dangers. The prevailing attitude during this period advocated stress reduction over stress management. In 1974, one of Sal's graduate students showed him a *Family Circle* magazine article that supported this position. It cautioned people against the perils of stressful experiences. The article even went so far as to suggest that people should avoid driving on heavily congested freeways whenever possible. Although most of us would like to avoid traffic congestion, getting to work and other important activities often rule out this option.

Sal's experience and research contradicted this article's ideas. His studies found that creative people regularly look for new, meaningful, and fulfilling experiences, some of which inevitably cause them stress. In many cases, such people perform some of their best work under great stress. Take Michelangelo, for example. He was unhappy when the Roman Catholic pope ordered him to leave Florence and his employer, the Medici family, for Rome to carve the Pietá and paint the Sistine Chapel's ceiling.[1]

Despite stressful work conditions and his desire to return to Florence, Michelangelo created marvels that the world still admires. This puzzling paradox led Sal and his researchers to the hypothesis that whether stressful changes enliven or destroy depends upon how one responds to them. They set out on a challenging research journey that resulted in discovering how hardiness promotes resilience.

THE ILLINOIS BELL TELEPHONE PROJECT

To test their hypothesis, Sal and his research team needed to study people who regularly experienced disruptive change. Sal turned to his friend Carl Horn, who was then an executive vice president at Illinois Bell Telephone (IBT) in Chicago, to see if IBT's managerial staff could participate in the study. Carl opened the doors to what would become a landmark study and a fundamental part of Sal's research into how different people handle stress. IBT's impending reorganization made it the right time to do such a study. At that point, American Telephone and Telegraph (AT&T) and its subsidiaries were a federally regulated monopoly. This immunity status eliminated both competition and dependence upon investors focusing on the bottom line. But, looking to speed up product and service advancements, external forces pressed toward open competition through deregulating "Ma Bell." This would pave the way for the telecommunication and Internet industries that we know today.

DEREGULATION AND DISRUPTION

In 1975, Sal and his research team began a twelve-year study paid for by IBT and the National Institute of Mental Health.[2] They evaluated roughly 450 male and female supervisors, managers, and decision makers at IBT, through yearly interviews, psychological tests, medical examinations, and work-performance reviews.

In 1981, six years into the study, the U.S. Federal Court ordered the earth-shattering deregulation of the "Ma Bell" monopoly. Deregulation changes dismantled IBT's long-standing policies and work norms in ways that greatly disrupted employees' functioning. Managers sometimes had as many as ten new supervisors within a twelve-month period. Neither they nor their supervisors had any real grasp of what was happening.

By the end of 1982, IBT had downsized from 26,000 to 14,000 employees. Some still regard the deregulation of AT&T as the largest upheaval in corporate history.

During this time, most IBT employees endured massive levels of stressful, disrupting changes. Close to half of the employees in our sample lost their jobs. Two-thirds of our sample broke down in various ways. Some had heart attacks or suffered depressive and anxiety disorders. Others abused alcohol and drugs, were separated and divorced, or acted out violently. In contrast, a third of our employee sample was resilient. These employees survived and thrived despite the stressful changes. If these individuals stayed at IBT, they rose to the top of the heap. If they left, they either started companies of their own or took strategically important employment in other companies.

THE ROOTS OF RESILIENCE

We studied our research data and IBT's employment records prior to the deregulation to see if there were differences in personality and coping style that distinguished the vulnerable from the resilient employees. That's how we discovered hardiness as the essence of resilience.

Prior to reorganization changes, the resilient IBT group's employment data agreed with our test data in illustrating telltale patterns of adaptable attitudes and skills the less resilient employees lacked. Measured through various relevant questionnaires and interviews, these resources surely helped in coping effectively with deregulation pressures. It makes sense that they fared better in performance, stamina, morale, conduct, and health, at work and at home, than did IBT's less resilient employees.

THREE RESILIENT ATTITUDES

Which attitudes distinguished the resilient employees in our study? Three key attitudes of *commitment*, *control*, and *challenge* came up repeatedly in the resilient group. We began to call them the 3Cs. These three attitudes combined to form a mindset of courage in the resilient employees. Through this, they could face the stressful changes and do the hard work of coping effectively with them.

Let's take a look at the specifics of these three attitudes:

1. COMMITMENT. When you are strong in the *commitment attitude*, you view your work as important and worthwhile enough to warrant your full attention, imagination, and effort. You stay involved with the events and people around you even when the going gets rough, and you sidestep unproductive alienating social behaviors, seeing withdrawal from stressful circumstances as weak.

2. CONTROL. When you are strong in the *control attitude*, you keep trying to positively influence the outcomes of the changes going on around you. Rather than let yourself sink into passivity and powerlessness, you do your best to find solutions to workday problems. In deciding where to apply your efforts, you determine which situational features are open to change and gracefully accept those outside of your control.

3. CHALLENGE. When you are strong in the *challenge attitude*, you see change as instrumental in opening up new, fulfilling pathways for living. You face up to stressful changes, try to understand

them, learn from them, and solve them. You embrace life's challenges, not deny and avoid them. This expresses your optimism toward the future rather than your fear of it.

TWO VITAL SKILLS

The courage and motivation of the three resilient attitudes bring about the skills of *transformational coping* and *social support*.

1. **TRANSFORMATIONAL COPING**. The resilient IBT employees transformed stressful changes to their advantage. First, they entered into a thought process that placed the changes into a broader perspective, taking the sting out of them, so to speak. A common way they broadened their perspective was to see a particular stress as happening to lots of other people. This made them feel less alone in their pain and struggle. As the broader perspectives made the stressful circumstances a bit more tolerable, they could then think about them long enough to deepen their understanding of them, which led to well-considered, innovative plans and problem-solving actions. This is a classic hands-on approach—get a firm grip on change and what it really means, then turn the situation to your advantage—as opposed to breaking down or acting precipitously in the face of change.

2. **SOCIAL SUPPORT**. In handling stressful changes in this direct manner, the resilient employees interacted by engaging others rather than by alienating them. They also attempted to resolve interpersonal work conflicts by interacting constructively, assisting and encouraging win-win solutions for all. They believed that problems are opportunities to strengthen relationships. Moreover, no matter how difficult things got, they sought to preserve relationship bridges because it was worthwhile and important to their growth.

A RESILIENT MANAGER

We interviewed Chuck repeatedly during the study. His attitudes and coping resources showed his resiliency and they stand as clear examples of what this book is meant to convey.

Although an engineer by trade, Chuck became an IBT customer relations manager. Prior to the deregulation, he exhibited the three resilient attitudes—commitment, control, and challenge—toward his work. This small, neat man in his midfifties introduced himself as someone who enjoys solving problems. His eyes lit up as he described customers' needs, investigating and mending customer disputes, and working out company service capabilities and obligations. He seemed to thrive on changes that made the most of his talents and capabilities. Chuck clearly anticipated the deregulation's more stressful aspects, but saw it as a stimulus to his and the company's growth.

1. THRIVING ON CHANGE

Shortly after the deregulation upheaval, Chuck said he experienced customer relations work as more challenging than before, although still manageable. Finding strategies to solve these new, professional challenges fascinated him. He astutely grasped customer concerns and problems arising from such changes. With greater marketplace competition, for example, customers had more places to take their business. Chuck knew that these customer concerns would emphasize his job position, making his role more central within the company. He also knew he needed more effective coping resources to handle the added pressures, and he formulated ideas to address these issues.

While many employees around him bemoaned the deregulation, and tried hard to hang on to the good-old days, Chuck looked to the future. He sought to understand the ways in which the deregulation would shift business concerns and practices and how this might open up new, prosperous ways of doing business. In particular, he anticipated that IBT would have to be much more proactive in order to retain its large customer base, now that it was competing with start-up companies. Rather than panicking about the deregulation and seeing it as a threat to IBT's business, he put it into perspective and saw it as a natural evolution of the telecommunications industry that could, in the end, work to everyone's advantage. He could now analyze the pros and cons more objectively, deepen his understanding, see ways to solve the problem, and act accordingly.

2. Taking Decisive Action

Chuck understood that the new competition in the telephone in- dustry probably meant an eventual decrease in the price of services for customers. But, he did not see this as the main area of his concern, as IBT was already offering rather low prices for services, not having had to worry about its bottom line. What seemed more immediately important to him was ensuring the satisfaction of IBT's customers with the services they were receiving, so that they would not switch to a competitor company.

To facilitate this goal, he set up an action plan that surveyed existing clients, to find out what they valued about their telephone services and what they wanted but did not have. The survey's tone was friendly, and it aimed at communicating to the customers IBT's strong interest in providing them with the best-possible ser- vice. The plan included maintaining the services that were valued, and in addition, working on providing or improving the services that were lacking or inadequate. To keep them on board, Chuck's plan included regular information updates as to the progress of the service improvements to customers.

Having gone this far in his deliberation, Chuck took his overall plan to his supervisors. Most of them were preoccupied by the swirling disruptions brought about by the deregulation, and had a difficult time taking his plan seriously. But, Chuck would not take "no" for an answer and persisted until his supervisors finally accepted that they needed to try to keep their customers happy, even though they were not happy themselves.

Finally, they adopted his plan, put him in charge of implementing it, and allocated the necessary resources to him. This effort paid off, as it became clear that customers appreciated what they saw as the company's loyalty to them and reacted in kind. Soon, the comments customers made about the improvements they desired began to drive IBT's research and development, ensuring its competitive success in the future. In this evolutionary process, Chuck became an increasingly central figure. He feels great about what has happened.

3. RESILIENCE AT HOME

Chuck also responsively attended to his family's needs, despite his strong commitment to work. His two children were just about to enter college. When they moved out of the family home, Chuck's wife planned to return to school to finish a college degree she had long ago interrupted. Although this change inconvenienced him, he supported his wife's personal development. Chuck considered ways in which they could maintain their loving, close relationship, despite spending less time together. He imagined involving himself in community organizations to make good use of his time alone.

4. LOOKING TO THE FUTURE

In the final interview, we asked Chuck to describe how he felt about the company's changes. He thought he would continue what he had started. He enjoys his work and wants to continue to help IBT to serve the public well. As to his family, he said, "I look forward to seeing my children marry, have children, and to my wife and I becoming grandparents."

Chuck liked his life as, all along, he pursued the goals he valued. "I enjoy a genuine life, full of challenges, meaning, and purpose, and look forward to more of it," he stated. Chuck rarely got ill, and although he was tired at the end of the day, he was content.

VULNERABILITY:
THE OPPOSITE OF RESILIENCE

Chuck was in the minority of our research sample. For every person like him, two people had poorer performance and health as the continuing stress overwhelmed them.

Even prior to the company deregulation, the nonresilient employees were vulnerable rather than hardy. They disengaged from stressful work events by avoiding and detaching from them as much as possible. They argued, "what good can possibly come about through change?" They had difficulty imagining how stressful circumstances could bring them anything other than pain. "Most things are out of your control," they'd say. They saw little reason to struggle.

These vulnerable employees lacked courage, motivation, and strategies to turn stressful changes to their advantage or grow in the process. Many of them waited for the dust to settle by downplaying or denying the significance or existence of changes. Choosing instead to distance themselves from stressful changes, these employees let unessential activities preoccupy them, or used vacation or sick days to escape their work responsibilities.

Some vulnerable employees exaggerated the impact stressful changes had on them. The more passive of these nonresilient employees felt like victims and tormented others through whining or complaints. Others, more aggressive, blamed workplace problems on their coworkers, supervisors, and employers. They competitively bolstered their self-esteem through emphasizing others' problems. In doing so, they sometimes tried to make others appear weak, foolish, and in need of their help. To them, this was easier than reaching out to others as equals.

As you probably have already surmised, the nonresilient employees fared badly in the company's efforts to deregulate and reorganize. They performed poorly, and frequent stress-related health problems compromised their job security. When there were personnel cuts, the company was most apt to terminate these less hardy employees.

ANDY B.:

A NONRESILIENT MANAGER

Among the managers we studied, Andy was clearly low in hardiness. In our various interviews with him, Andy, a carefully groomed and dressed forty-three-year-old, sat stiffly at his desk, alert and ready to answer our questions. His eagerness to please, and his polite and proper behavior, made him appear younger than his chronological age.

As a residential-telephone service line manager, Andy turned upper management directives into job orders for his subordinates. He precisely described his job as predictable and unchanging in routine. "I'm a link in the chain of command," he stated, "I know each day what I have to do and how to do it." He worried about workplace unruliness that would accompany the deregulation.

When the deregulation hit, the many changes disrupted workplace procedures and goals, and flying by the seat of one's pants became the company norm. At that point, Andy's worry turned to fear. His growing responsibilities required more creativity on his part. He was less and less efficient, and at times, confused about what to do next. Andy yearned for the good-old days of more precise company objectives and plans. Job security now weighed heavily upon him. He worried about his performance and hoped supervisors still thought well of him.

To allay the threat, Andy lost himself in his work. He sometimes wished for early retirement, especially in the hope of return-ing to normal home life. At home, he spoke of nothing else except work problems, and despite his wife's reassurance and comfort, he still felt anxious and worried almost all the time. Although he appreciated her efforts, he also blamed her for insufficiently at-tending to his needs. When he felt most out of control, he verbally struck out against her, and felt very guilty for doing so. "I hate hurting her," he stated.

Andy's parental responsibilities overwhelmed him as well. "Al-though my children do well," he stated, "they still need my help and guidance." He doubted that he was up to parenting them dur-ing the stressful times he had to endure.

When we asked Andy about his future plans, he had little to say. Thinking that far ahead disturbed him, but if pressed to re-spond, he disliked appearing vulnerable and out of control. He wished for more predictable work situations in order to prove his worth.

Andy let work problems influence how he felt about himself, which took a toll on his health. On health questionnaires, Andy reported irritability, insomnia, heart palpitations, and periods of appetite loss. Routine health tests, provided by IBT's medical de-partment, showed increases in Andy's heart rate and blood pres-sure, and following the deregulation, he developed a stomach ulcer.

SUMMARY

Here you have two clear-cut case studies of the different sides of resilience at work. Chuck W. survived and thrived during the IBT upheaval through his strong hardiness—his attitudes of commit-ment, control, and challenge, and his well-developed coping skills. He is a good example of what we are talking about in this book. On the other hand, Andy B. had little resilience to begin with and his ability to cope evaporated completely in the face of stressful changes.

We have learned a lot since those early years at IBT, especially about how hardiness works to preserve one's performance, health, morale, and conduct. Back then, we had some idea of the need for hardiness in the workplace but were less aware of its broader meaning and application.

CHAPTER 3

HOW HARDINESS PROMOTES RESILIENCE

As we've seen, resilience is the capacity to survive and thrive despite stressful circumstances. But some people do it far better than others, so we need to look for pathways to resilience. The initial twelve-year study at IBT uncovered that hardiness is revealed in a pattern of attitudes and skills that promote resilience. Hardiness preserves people's performance and health by helping them to think and act constructively when stressful circumstances occur.

STRESS CAN BUILD UP

There are two kinds of stress. One involves disruptive changes in routine or circumstance. For example, your boss suddenly tells you that a cut in your department budget will change how you operate, and at the most extreme, that you may not have a job. This *acute stress*, though disruptive to you, is time limited and has clear parameters. You may get a call to pick up an ill child from school, have to work overtime to cover work-task responsibilities for another employee on vacation, or the company may ask you to forgo a yearly bonus because of economic pressures. Whether big or small, acute daily changes like these call for us to act, and thus temporarily disrupt our work.

The other kind of stress involves ongoing disparities between what you want and what you get. Maybe you are stuck in a routine job that rarely allows you to use your true creative capabilities. Your job pays the bills, but satisfies you very little. This *chronic stress* festers and may magnify when stressful changes appear.

The weight of acute and chronic stress on your performance, health, morale, and conduct depends upon their amount and intensity. The less chronic stress you have, the more acute stress you can handle, and vice versa. If, for example, you find a close fit between what you want and what you do or get, you are more apt to smoothly navigate acute stressful changes. If, on the other hand, you really dislike what you do or get, any acute change will throw you for a loop.

Your total stress level, then, is a combination of the amount and intensity of the acute and chronic stress in your life. The greater your total stress, the more it can undermine you physically, mentally, and behaviorally.

CIVILIZED EXPRESSIONS OF THE FIGHT-OR-FLIGHT RESPONSE

Your mind tends to respond to stressful circumstances as dangers you must protect yourself against. In this process, the mind mobilizes the body to attack the danger, or run away from it. This, well-known fight-or-flight response to stress involves a physical mobilization that arouses both body and mind.[1] To quicken brain and body responses, adrenaline pumps into your blood stream and stored fat deposits turn into sugar for energy. Your digestive and immune systems also suppress, as there is little time in dealing with dangers for niceties, like food digestion and protection against infections.

The fight-or-flight response was very appropriate early in human history. In less-civilized times, our typical stress involved competitive encounters with animals or other human beings over survival means, like food or shelter. If these animals or human beings overpowered us physically, there was little to do but fight or run away. If we won the battle or successfully ran away, our body arousal decreased. We then returned to normal activities until the next encounter.

The emergence of civilized social norms made the fight-or-flight response less adaptive. First, we typically no longer encounter dangers such as wild animals and human predators. Second, social values, standards, and laws restrict us from fighting and running away. Today, the root of our acute and chronic stress is social, typically work and personal changes, and conflicts that disrupt the status quo and affect us psychologically and socially. Although some acute stress is clearly negative, such as job demotions and automobile accidents, some can have both positive and negative features, such as company reorganizations, job promotions, and the birth of a new baby. Chronic stress typically involves a lack of something desired, like intimacy or creative work. If we respond to such stress by fighting or running away, others may view us as out of control, irresponsible, weak, ineffective, or some other unflattering attribute. Instead, we try to cope with stressful circumstances by rising responsibly to these tension-filled occasions.

Our modern mind still registers acute and chronic stress as danger. This is true even for stress that is not life threatening. If stress remains unchanged by our coping efforts, our bodies stay mobilized. If prolonged, this mobilization undermines our performance, morale, conduct, and health. We call this prolonged fight-or-flight response *strain* to emphasize how disadvantageous it is to our overall well-being.

MODERATING YOUR STRAIN LEVEL

Unless you are careful, unresolved stressful circumstances can result in physical, mental, and behavioral symptoms. *Physical strain* can include symptoms like muscle tension, backaches, fatigue, anxiety, stomach and intestinal upsets, colds and flus, and other physical irregularities. *Mental strain* can include symptoms like irritability, impatience, impaired memory and forgetfulness, poor concentration and attention, sadness, pessimism, depression, and other mental irregularities. And, *behavioral strain* can include symptoms like sleep problems, temper outbursts, social distancing, poor performance, socially insensitive actions, and other behavioral irregularities. These various strain symptoms, if prolonged, can result in degenerative wear-and-tear health problems, like heart attacks, strokes, cancer, and diabetes.

Intense and prolonged strain increases your likelihood for breakdowns in work performance, as well. In times of strain, you may insufficiently complete work tasks and fail to meet deadlines. You may also find it difficult to behave responsibly and supportively toward others. Without intending to, you may decrease job promotion opportunities, or at the most extreme, court job termination.

At home, you may distance yourself from family members, preferring isolation to their company. Your own problems may also occupy you so much that you communicate less and less with family members and show little interest in nurturing them. If these problems persist, you risk relationship breakdowns that at the most extreme can end in divorce.

CONFRONTING STRESS HEAD-ON

Fortunately, there is a way out of this sinister scenario. To ensure sound performance, health, morale, and conduct in rapidly changing times, you must find and use more civilized and socially relevant ways to cope with problems than fighting or running away. Hardiness helps you to do this.

Specifically, the resilient attitudes of commitment, control, and challenge give you the necessary courage and motivation to search for constructive, civilized ways of decreasing the stressfulness of circumstances around you. Through these decisive attitudes, you temper less socially responsible reactions to stress and replace them, instead, with constructive thinking and actions.

This courage and motivation helps you to exercise the coping skill of solving, rather than avoiding problems, and the social interaction skill of giving and getting assistance and encouragement. These hardy skills further guarantee a resilient outcome. Through these key skills, you act in ways that turn stressful circumstances into opportunities, and give and receive help from others in this process.

The hardier IBT employees showed great resilience. Rather than succumb to company changes, like their less-resilient comrades, they survived and thrived, despite IBT's immense organizational changes. Many people already possess such coping and social interaction skills, although their ability to use these skills varies. If, however, you lack the necessary attitudes and skills to cope resiliently with life's problems, you can learn and develop them.

ADDITIONAL HARDINESS RESEARCH

The clear message of the IBT study is that, in order to be resilient under stressful changes, you must have hardiness. Since the time of that study, hardiness has made a big splash among researchers and practitioners alike. By now, there are more than six hundred research studies on hardiness around the world. The questionnaire used in these studies measures the attitudes of commitment, control, and challenge, and the skills of coping by solving problems and interacting by giving and receiving assistance and encouragement. These measures have provoked the questions you will be asked in chapters 5, 7, and 9, in order to assess your own hardiness. Ongoing hardiness research continually shows its role in promoting resiliency to be consistent with the IBT findings. These studies have evaluated stressful changes across many different kinds of people and circumstances. In addition, the people studied ranged in age, income, educational level, gender, ethnicity, race, and job characteristics. Examples include not only the usual disruptive changes of company reorganizations, but also the culture shock of working abroad or emigrating, pressure of sports competition, uncertainty of leaving home to go to college, grief from nursing dying patients, pain of divorce proceedings and family breakups, and danger of life-threatening circumstances.

The overall conclusion is that hardiness enhances performance, conduct, leadership, stamina, and health under stressful, changing circumstances. Here are some of the other consistent findings that underscore the main conclusion:

- People with highly developed resilient attitudes—the 3Cs—perceive stressful circumstances to be less threatening.

- The more resilient people are, the more likely they are to complete tasks in creative ways rather than in routine ways.

- Dealing head-on with stressful circumstances in creative ways results in less physical, mental, and behavioral strain.

- Hardiness is an amalgam of resilient attitudes, coping skills, support-enhancing social interactions, and behaviors.

Resiliency has been studied in a wide range of life activities. The greater detail that follows will give you some idea of the extent and importance of what has been found out in the research.

LIFE-THREATENING STRESS

Several studies assessed hardiness levels of U.S. military personnel before they went abroad on either combat missions, such as the Gulf War, or peacekeeping missions, such as Bosnia.[2] Military personnel experienced life-threatening stress on both types of missions. Even on peacekeeping missions, opposing forces shot at, bombed, and sabotaged military personnel. There were also lots of other disruptive changes in both types of missions. These disruptions included leaving family and home, unpredictable circumstances, and having to deal with whatever came up in threatening, unfamiliar overseas contexts.

Upon the troops' return to the United States, researchers evaluated them for signs of physical and mental breakdown that are inconsistent with resiliency. They also had medical and performance active-duty service records for these troops. The results showed that military personnel who had higher levels of questionnaire-measured hardy attitudes before they left on the missions were better protected from breaking down into depressive and posttraumatic stress disorders following their experience of life-threatening, battlefield stress. This finding is consistent with the view that the hardiness to manage stressful circumstances and solve the problems they represent provides the courage and capability to be resilient.

PHYSICAL AND MENTAL HEALTH

There are also numerous research studies documenting that hardiness protects physical and mental health under stressful conditions that are not life threatening.[3] As a group, the studies cover both genders, a wide range of ages, other demographics, and circumstances. In addition, the studies have involved people from various cultures. Typically, the studies include questionnaire measures of hardiness, symptoms of mental and/or physical illness, and the stressfulness of circumstances.

The results are quite consistent. The more stressful circumstances become, the greater the signs of physical and/or mental illnesses. Hardiness, however, moderates this absence of resilience. The higher your hardiness level, the less likely you are to get physical or mental symptoms when you experience stressful circumstances.

A few studies also address how the protective effect of hardiness takes place.[4] They have shown that the higher your hardiness level, the milder your physiological arousal to stressful circumstances. They used as signs of arousal blood pressure and heart rate readings and the presence of stress-induced hormones, like cortisol. Strong physiological reactions to stresses predispose you to various kinds of health breakdown. This is even more reason to approach the rigors of daily living with a strong hardiness level that will lead to resilience.

COMPETITIVE SPORTS

In another study, researchers measured the levels of hardy attitudes, coping, and supportive interactions of female swimmers before they competed with each other for a place on the U.S. women's 2000 Olympic synchronized swimming team.[5] The swimmers, and their coaches, did not know their hardiness levels prior to the competition, since the results were not made available. The ten women highest in hardiness made the final cut for the team. Then, in the actual Olympic competition, the team tied with that of another country, which led to a runoff match, to see which team would make the finals. In this match, the other country's team won. Interestingly, the two U.S. swim team members who faltered during this decisive match had the lowest hardiness levels on the U.S. team. These results suggest that hardiness helps participating team members to maintain their resilience in competitions, especially when they need precise synchronous efforts to thrive.

Less dramatic, though similar in its results, is a study of hardiness and performance in male high school varsity basketball players in Southern California.[6] Researchers tested the hardiness levels of these players by questionnaire prior to their fall playing season. They then obtained season data on these players' basketball performance from their coaches. The researchers organized these data into seven signs of performance effectiveness, such as number of points scored, assists, rebounds, free throws, foul outs, and number of minutes played in games won. On six of the seven signs, hardiness predicted good performance. Only the number of free throws made failed to predict hardiness level. When you stop to think about this, free throws are the only performance sign that tends to involve a period of relative calm (except, of course, in crucial last-minute situations). The whistle blows; you step to the line and throw an unobstructed shot that, for a varsity player, is a well-practiced, routine activity. With all the other effectiveness measures that emphasize tumultuous and unpredictable circumstances, hardiness level predicted good performance. This study, too, shows that hardiness helps you to be resilient in stressfully competitive circumstances.

LEADERSHIP QUALITIES

A study done at West Point Military Academy attempted to understand what qualities make cadets effective leaders.[7] The academy encourages its cadets to be leaders, both in ongoing course work and in their various community-outreach activities. The academy measures leadership skills in various ways, especially the psychological and social factors that influence the development or absence of these skills. The researchers measured these psychosocial factors, including hardiness, shortly after a cohort of cadets arrived at the academy. They measured leadership at various times during the cadets' stay.

It turned out that hardiness was the best predictor of leadership behavior over the four years of the cadets' training program. The specific leadership signs included becoming a model for their cadet peers, helping their peers bring out the best in themselves, and taking the initiative in performing community services. These results are quite consistent with other studies on hardiness and leadership.[8] We would expect this, as courage, initiative, and the ability to solve problems and build teams are qualities of leadership.

COLLEGE PERFORMANCE

Several college performance studies evaluate the influence of hardiness on college students' performance and retention.[9] Hardiness, measured by a questionnaire given just before the students enrolled in college, turns out to be a better predictor of retention than are either Scholastic Aptitude Test (SAT) scores or class rank in high school. These results that show hardiness as critical to school retention are particularly interesting since SAT scores and graduating rank in high school are currently the major criteria used by colleges in evaluating student applications.

Another study shows how high school graduates cope with the anticipatory stress of entering college, in the summer prior to their enrollment. Researchers measured these students' hardiness levels by questionnaire during college orientation week.[10] They also performed urine screen tests on them to detect recent alcohol and drug use. The results show that hardy people are less likely to try to cope with stressful circumstances by using alcohol and drugs.

STRESSFUL WORK CONTEXTS

Several studies of stressful work environments evaluated levels of stress and hardiness among nurses, such as those assisting in hospital operating rooms and taking care of dying people in hospice settings.[11] In such settings, nurses high in hardiness take fewer sick days and show less depression, anxiety, and burnout.

Similarly, the higher firefighters' levels of hardiness are, the less stressed they feel, and the greater fulfillment and meaning they find in their job.[12]

There is also a two-year study of American computer specialists in China on a training mission.[13] The researcher measured the specialists' levels of hardiness by questionnaire before they left the United States. In the first six months of their mission, the entire training group experienced culture shock sufficient to impede their job performance and undermine their health. They had concentration and memory difficulties, tendencies toward social isolation, anxiety, and depression, and a range of physical symptoms. In the remaining year and a half, however, those who were high in hardiness became more resilient, showing performance and health levels equal, if not better, than before they left the United States. In contrast, those who were low in hardiness recovered more slowly, if at all. Those specialists whom the company sent home due to poor performance had low levels of hardiness.

Hardiness also enhances employees' performance in entrepreneurial jobs, which tend to be stressful because, to be successful, you must develop, market, and service your products. In one particular study, researchers evaluated levels of hardiness in the entrepreneurial effectiveness of consultants.[14] Billable hours, that is, the number of service hours charged to their clients, showed how well these consultants performed in their tasks of developing and servicing their clients. The results showed clearly that the higher the consultant's hardiness level, the greater the number of billable hours over the course of two years.

——————— SUMMARY ———————

Where does resilience come from? A massive body of research supports the importance of hardiness to performance and health under stressful, changing circumstances. We have applied what we learned from this scientific evidence to servicing individuals and organizations interested in resilient performance, health, morale, and conduct. In this process, we perfected our test for measuring people's hardiness, and have extrapolated from it the questions posed to you in chapters 5, 7, and 9 about your own hardiness. Today, many companies, military and safety organizations, and schools use our hardiness test to screen applicants as to their resilience and to identify strengths and weaknesses in existing personnel. We often follow up this test by teaching hardiness procedures for enhancing resilience in these settings. Now we would like to teach these same principles to you so that you can learn *Resilience at Work*.

CHAPTER 4

YOU CAN *LEARN*
TO BE RESILIENT

Resilient people seem so capable that it is easy to think they were born that way. Certainly, some youngsters do show early signs of hardiness. Think of youngsters eager to learn everything and interested in everything around them, as compared to youngsters less involved in life. But, even if hardier adults report enthusiastic and purposeful childhoods, it may be a mistake to conclude that genes determine resiliency. After all, we know that some people emerge as hardy only later in their development. So where does resilience come from?

EARLY EXPERIENCES THAT
BUILD RESILIENCE

Our early IBT research gave us clues to the origins of hardiness. Years later, Debbie analyzed IBT's employee interview data, as to early conditions that differentiated the resilient and nonresilient employee groups.[1] Researchers in the early study were blind to the employee hardiness levels of those with whom they interacted.

- **EARLY STRESS.** Interestingly, many of the employees who tested high in hardiness reported stressful early lives. Their stress included serious illnesses in themselves or family members, single-parent households, divorces, financial difficulties, unemployment, alcoholism or substance abuse in family members, and frequent, disruptive changes in residence. These early lives if anything were more stressful than reported by those employees low in hardiness.

- **SENSE OF PURPOSE.** Another important feature of those high in resilience is that many of them recalled their parents' singling them out as special in some important way. Talents, skills, maturity, or other unique, defining features contributed to parents elevating these children's role within the family. As such, the parents supported these youngsters' capabilities through either encouraging their gifts and talents or assigning them family responsibilities, or both. These children developed a keen sense of purposeful direction in school, community, and work activities. In contrast to less determined youngsters, these children emerged hardier, responsive to growth-promoting opportunities, and creative in carving out niches that fully expressed themselves.

- **NURTURED CONFIDENCE.** In school, teachers or other adults spotted and nurtured these youngsters. This helped their confidence. These youngsters' openness to and involvement with the environment must have gotten their teachers' attention. In any event, the high-resilience employees had found learning stimulating and fun. They further expected their efforts to lead to good results and cherished their central roles at home and at school. When these hardier youngsters encountered personal frustrations or setbacks, they utilized the help and encouragement of others.

What exactly did the resilient IBT employees learn about themselves in their youth? They learned that they were important enough to fully engage in living (*commitment attitude*), they could influence positively much of what happens to them (*control attitude*), and they could use ongoing changes in ways that benefited their development and growth (*challenge attitude*). Their hardy attitudes helped them to embrace life and to develop resources to cope effectively with life's circumstances.

EARLY EXPERIENCES
THAT UNDERMINE RESILIENCE

In contrast, the nonresilient employees remembered their childhood experiences differently.

- **LITTLE FAMILY ENCOURAGEMENT.** Some recalled parents who rigidly advocated to them about rules, values, and family norms. They recalled few times, if any, when their parents made them feel especially capable or talented. If they did, however, it was inconsistent, oftentimes the result of external pressures rather than personal sentiment. Many within this group only vaguely recalled meaningful family interactions and attributed much of this to outside preoccupations that undermined family functioning. For various reasons, in their youth, these adults recalled limited encouragement, help, and empathy from their parents. They also reported that, before long, they began hiding their feelings, frustrations, and problems from their parents.

- **NO SENSE OF PURPOSE.** The nonresilient employees insufficiently appreciated how school and other community activities served as stepping stones to a fulfilling life. Vaguely defined talents and goals undermined their ability to grasp the larger picture.

- **LACK OF INVOLVEMENT.** As children, this group also shied away from teachers. They did what they could to get by in school, with little sense of involvement or influence. Even though some of them did well academically, they still felt socially inadequate. These employees reported more unhappiness at home and at school than their more resilient co-workers.

As you can see, the nonresilient IBT employees did not have hardy attitudes and skills. As youngsters, they learned early to avoid life's problems (*alienation as opposed to commitment*), to refrain from influencing the manageable aspects of change (*powerlessness as opposed to control*), and to fear changes that disrupt stability (*threat as opposed to challenge*). These self-defeating attitudes toward living prevented them from coping and interacting effectively under pressure.

CAN RESILIENCE BE LEARNED IN CHILDHOOD?

Genetic inheritance affects our performance and health on many levels, but you can learn resilience as a child. There are many examples of people, genetically disadvantaged and thus vulnerable, who have nonetheless overcome such limitations, sometimes in extraordinary ways. In contrast, there are also just as many examples of people who, though apparently well-endowed genetically, are surprisingly low in hardiness.[2]

Our IBT employee-history interviews showed how early experiences can be a formative influence on resilience. The development of hardy attitudes and skills in children varies with certain characteristics of their environment and parental interaction. What is the gist of this childhood hardiness? Circumstances that provide children with opportunities to find purpose, direction, and meaning in dealing with stressful changes strengthen resilient attitudes and resources within them. The resilient IBT employees' early losses, setbacks, supportive parenting, and teachings gave them numerous opportunities to learn how to turn change to advantage and to use constructively the support from which to accomplish this.

CAN YOU LEARN RESILIENCE IN ADULTHOOD?

As long as you can use life experiences to grow, psychologically and socially, you can learn to be resilient as an adult. Resist falling into the trap of thinking that once you reach adulthood, you are what you are, and nothing will change that. Hardiness research, detailed below, indicates that adolescents and adults can learn to be resilient.

HARDINESS TRAINING

Our efforts to foster hardiness in adults began at IBT, in the years following the deregulation upheavals. IBT decision makers came to us, indicating that they knew us as careful and determined researchers, but wondered if we could also help their employees to become more resilient. The company was then in the throes of massive downsizing and reorganization, with the aim of being competitive in the new telecommunications industry. These upheavals were taking a great toll on the employees, and they needed hardiness badly.

In the first practical application of our research, we put together a hardiness training program based on our findings about hardiness we had found in the resilient group and the parent/child relationships they had reported.[3] Specifically, we devised techniques and exercises to help trainees handle stressful circumstances by turning them to advantage (rather than by avoiding or attacking them) and to help them interact with others by giving and receiving assistance and encouragement (rather than by deepening ongoing conflicts). Also, we included ways to use the feedback from these efforts to deepen the attitudes of commitment, control, and challenge. In addition, the trainers tried to give the encouragement and support to trainees implementing the techniques and exercises that the resilient employees in our research sample had reported getting from their parents. As you will see later, the training was effective in helping trainees learn hardy coping, social interaction, and attitudes. It is this training procedure that has led to the exercises you will encounter in chapters 6, 8, and 10. The beleaguered IBT employees benefited greatly from this training. The abiding emphasis of our hardiness training program is on transformational coping and supportive social interactions and using these to deepen the attitudes of commitment, control, and challenge.

- ■ TRANSFORMATIONAL COPING. Through mental and behavioral actions, you transform the features of stressful changes and use them to advantage. At the *mental level*, stressful circumstances are placed into broader perspectives, so they can be managed more easily. An example is the time perspective, which may help you realize that the deadlines are all this week, so that next week you can get back to normal. You also learn how to deepen your understanding of problems, so you know what to do to solve them. An example is the recognition that the stress is based on unfortunate but resolvable misunderstandings between you and your boss. At the *action level*, mental insights are used to plan and carry out decisive courses of problem-solving actions. The feedback gained from carrying out these activities deepens your hardy attitudes of commitment, control, and challenge. This process leads to greater resilience under stress.

- ■ SUPPORTIVE SOCIAL INTERACTIONS. The other abiding emphasis of our hardiness training program strives to foster supportive interactions that can help solve problems. Here, you identify and resolve ongoing conflicts that exist between you and others, and replace them with patterns of sharing assistance and encouragement. In doing this, you learn communication, listening, and behavior skills that bring about supportive interactions to improve relationships. Often, the trainee has to take the first steps unilaterally in trying to improve the relationships. The training process helps you to both understand and accept this approach, by realizing that if you are helpful to a coworker, it will be difficult for him or her not to respond in kind.

Trainees practice these coping and support skills in real-life circumstances and use the feedback they get from their efforts to deepen their hardy attitudes. They emerge with the knowledge and skills to turn potentially disruptive stresses into advantages. Once the program is over, they have developed the courage, motivation, and strategies to approach stressful circumstances resiliently.

■ GAUGING THE RESULTS. By now, there are a number of research studies of working adults and college students, all of which show the effectiveness of this type of resiliency training. The general pattern of the studies uses questionnaires to measure the hardiness levels in the participants before the training begins and after it is over. In addition, we measure their job or school performance in relevant ways, before and after training. To clarify the relative effectiveness of our training program, we further compare the participants to people who receive other special training or no training at all.

At IBT, we compared IBT employees going through hardiness training to other IBT employees still on the training wait list.[4] Those who had completed the training were hardier, performed better on the job, were more satisfied with their job, and had a greater sense of personal fulfillment than those still on the waiting list. Their stress, strain, anxiety, depression, and blood pressure also simultaneously decreased, and their supervisors' performance evaluations of them improved. These group differences persisted over the six months following the end of the training program.

There have been other studies of hardiness training for working adults who are undergoing great changes. When these adults went through specific training for hardiness, as compared to other adult trainees who received more conventional stress-management training, the results matched those already discussed. These other studies of similar training programs reinforce the value and effectiveness of hardiness training.[5]

When we do hardiness training in the workplace, we typically arrange for there to be an "alumni" meeting, roughly one month after the training is over. This is an opportunity for trainees to meet once again, share what has been happening to them after the training, and fill out a questionnaire about how the training has affected them. Across the various groups, 90 percent of the working adults find the training of marked value and 93 percent feel that they have definitely improved in their ability to deal with stressful circumstances.

By now, there are also research studies of hardiness training with college students.[6] In these, the training for resilience is offered as a regular credit course for students who need or want it. These courses offer similar training to that used for working adults, and show similar results. Not only does questionnaire-based hardiness increase as students go through the course, so too do their grade-point averages and retention in school over the next two years.

Taken together, these research findings on the effectiveness of hardiness training show a number of beneficial results that persist over time:

- Trainees become more imaginative about how to bridge the gap between their needs and those of their company and co-workers. They are no longer overcome with panic, anger, and detachment.

- They feel more self-confident, as they think through all the changes that are taking place. They no longer feel inadequate and vulnerable.

- They feel more energetic and enthusiastic on a day-to-day basis. They have fewer headaches, upset stomachs, aches and pains, and don't have trouble getting out of bed anymore.

- They feel more involved in the events going on around them, and think they can really make a difference. They don't think of themselves as victims being preyed upon by those in power.

- They have a sense of a better future for themselves, rather than thinking it is only other people that can get what they want in life.

- They procrastinate and avoid less, and do less stress-related eating and drinking.

- As they come to feel less overwhelmed and powerless, they cut corners and disregard rules less.

- They feel more flexible, and open to whatever happens. It is less likely that they get stuck in old beliefs about how the world works, as they become more open to possibilities and how they can actually improve their lives.

SUMMARY

Developing resilience in people is our life's work. We enjoy helping people to improve their hardiness and, as a consequence, to enhance their performance, health, morale, and conduct. It seems clear from the research on adolescents and adults that you can learn hardiness; it is not just in the genes. In this chapter, we have presented a rough outline of what our training program involves. In the pages that follow, we will take you through our specific training techniques that will help you to navigate successfully whatever work changes come your way.

CHAPTER 5

DO YOU HAVE THE RIGHT ATTITUDES TO THRIVE IN ADVERSITY?

"When one door of happiness closes, another opens; but often we look so long at the closed door that we do not see the one which has been opened for us."

—HELEN KELLER[1]

Most of us today can imagine a workplace undergoing disruptive changes. Perhaps you work in such a place right now. When a company is reorganizing to meet budget pressures or market opportunities, when there are layoffs, mergers, and shifts in job definition, employees often feel like there is nothing, and no one, they can count on anymore. Work changes may worry and preoccupy them so much that they have little interest or time to nurture satisfying work relationships. In a rapidly changing workplace supervisors are often less and less accessible, and when they finally do have time, they may be less candid and supportive about goings-on. Employees may no longer recognize the company and coworkers they once knew. Unpredictable work environments and fewer self-development opportunities make it increasingly difficult to feel good about your work and yourself. Job insecurity, arising from a possible termination or a possible transfer, arising from new supervisors and shifting career paths, is today's most frequently cited employee concern.[2]

We all strive to gain mastery and predictability over our environment. We differ, however, in the ways we react to our fear of change. It's difficult to completely eliminate the fear that comes with stressful changes, but you can learn to manage it and do what needs to be done anyway.

By opening up to life's changes through attitudes that marshal your coping resources, you can seize creative, satisfying, and interesting opportunities. The following three attitudes position you to embrace change resiliently.

A CLOSER LOOK AT THE 3Cs

As the IBT study first revealed, hardy attitudes—attitudes of commitment, control, and challenge—give you the courage and motivation to turn stressful changes to your advantage. These three attitudes are the key to resilience and must be learned and mastered. Now let's examine them more closely.

COMMITMENT

"Life exacts a price for less-than-full participation in it. We lose touch with human values and qualities that arise naturally from a full engagement with work and life that expresses responsibility, integrity, loyalty, and cooperation."
—TARTHANG TULKU[3]

The attitude of commitment helps you to engage fully in work tasks and life. You are committed to the importance of your job, your family, and all of your life's pursuits. It is your involvement with the people and events going on around you that lends meaning and fulfillment to your life. You stay involved to the best of your ability and continue to do so no matter how stressful the circumstances.

Your dedication to an activity arises from your belief system and influences how you cope with stressful changes in key ways. When you appraise the people and activities in your life as important to your personal satisfaction and system of meaning, and your interaction with them as worthwhile enough to pursue vigorously, you are more apt to commit and dedicate yourself to them both in will and action.

This attitude also applies to situations and circumstances. Your attitude of commitment shapes your understanding of the events around you and is the basis for evaluating situational outcomes. You ask yourself, "Do I have the interest to solve this problem?" If so, you are more apt to dedicate yourself to it. In this circumstance, your attitude of commitment is high. If the opposite is true, however, you are more apt to deny or avoid the problem to minimize its damage to you.

The reactions Charlie and George had to their company's reorganization shows the importance of commitment. In its decentralization effort, the company's headquarters, where both men work, is downsizing considerably. Strong in commitment, Charlie wants to stay involved with the work and his coworkers, and keeps thinking through what is happening, asking others how they feel and how they're doing. He keeps working on things and participating as much as, if not more than, before the downsizing. He continues to care about the company and its members. In contrast, George sees the reorganization as just another disruption. With little commitment, he quickly concludes that the company decision makers are incompetent and not worth his loyalty, and that his fellow employees are fools not to see this. He detaches himself from everything that is going on and does as little as possible during the workday, preferring to lose himself in daydreams of more enjoyable times.

CONTROL

"Lack of willpower has caused more failure than lack of intelligence or ability."
—FLOWERS A. NEWHOUSE[4]

The attitude of control enables you to take direct, hands-on action to transform changes and the problems they may cause. This attitude helps you believe that stressful changes are important and worthwhile enough to dedicate yourself to influencing them in an advantageous direction. You are likely to say, "Let me find, or develop, the resources to solve this problem." Sufficient personal coping resources make it easier for you to influence the outcome of the problem. If you believe that you can influence the outcome of a stressful change (control attitude), you are more apt to push yourself to cope with it. Of course, how much and in which direction you can influence changes varies from one situation to the next.

The strength and direction of your coping efforts depend upon your estimation of the likelihood of bringing about positive change. An attitude of control heightens this estimation, which mobilizes and sustains your coping efforts in the face of adversity. The added benefit is that this coping effort in turn strengthens your commitment attitude as well. Through your unremitting dedication to solving the task, you do what you can to make things turn out well.

If the opposite is true, you may question your ability to turn stressful changes around and stop trying. Remember, however, that though it helps to have an accommodating environment that supports your coping efforts, you should try to influence change positively even in less supportive circumstances.

Keep in mind that there are some things in work and life that we simply cannot control. An important aspect of evaluating the features of a stressful change is assessing what is and is not possible. Some circumstances only permit change within us. You then need greater ingenuity and effort to move change in positive directions. The greatest personal change can happen in such circumstances. If you are high in the attitude of control, you fully grasp the directions in which life's changes push you, events, and others.

The importance of an attitude of control can been seen in the experiences of Linda and Allison. Both women work for a company that is being acquired by another, larger firm, and are experiencing all the reorganizational turmoil this brings. Linda gulps twice and throws herself into thinking through the likely implications of the changes for her, for those around her, and for the company itself. She also tries to anticipate what additional changes may be coming. Through all of this, she keeps in her mind the downside of the changes, and the upside as well, and what she can do to influence beneficial outcomes. This attitude helps her take action to cope and interact in relevant, effective ways. By contrast, Allison panics and has a sense of powerlessness as the changes mount. She does not believe it likely that she can do anything constructive, so she tries to decrease her pain by detaching herself from what is happening. She concludes that whatever is going to happen will happen, so it is better to think that it doesn't matter to her anyway. Whenever she is unsuccessful in detaching herself, her increasing anxiety gives way to anger, as she sees herself as the victim of the powerful and wealthy people who don't care at all about her.

CHALLENGE

"Our greatest glory is not in never failing,
but in rising up every time we fail."
—RALPH WALDO EMERSON[5]

The attitude of challenge lets you embrace change as a normal life process. You take an unbiased stance toward change that develops your "taste" for what satisfies you on a long-term basis. Positive and negative experiences are simply grist for the learning mill. This does not mean that you jump for joy when stressful changes come your way. Instead, you approach change as a meaningful challenge by seeing opportunity in every difficulty, rather than by seeing it the other way around.

If you are strong in the attitude of challenge, then you stay motivated despite stressful changes, are especially able to learn from your disappointments to do better the next time, and maintain that whatever does not kill you makes you stronger. Change is a necessary stimulus for self-discovery and growth, and provides you opportunity to further develop purpose and meaning.

People who are high in the challenge attitude are very different from those who are low. Take the example of Bernice and Oliver, managers in a high-tech company that was increasingly going into the red. Bernice regrets the decisions, some of which she had participated in, that led the company on its downward spiral. But, she feels the company can learn from these failures, and she keeps struggling to see alternatives that could improve the situation. Instead of panicking, she tries to see how to do better, assuming that there is a lot to be learned. In contrast, Oliver sees the failures as an unchangeable sign of his and the company's inadequacy. He is overwhelmed with the pain of what is happening, and fearfully wants to keep it from becoming public. This leads him to entertain ways of covering up the financial mess, even if that means lying about it and breaking rules.

HOW ATTITUDES INFLUENCE RESILIENCE

What is a person like when all three hardy attitudes are high or low at the same time? If they are all high, the person is courageous and motivated to take advantage of changes, however stressful they may be. This is the pathway to resilience. In contrast, if the attitudes are all low, the person is fearful and vulnerable, without any strength or motivation to confront stressful circumstances. The examples that follow show this difference.

THE COURAGE AND MOTIVATION FOR RESILIENCE

You may be familiar with the television sitcom *Cheers*, with its appealing and quirky characters played by an outstanding, diverse cast of actors and actresses. John Ratzenberger's background was of particular interest to us, especially with regard to hardiness. Prior to playing Cliff on *Cheers*, he was a starving, unemployed actor residing in England. Thirty-something and down-and-out, John's uneventful career had been sprinkled with minor acting jobs. John was literally a step away from homelessness when, in 1982, he came upon the *Cheers* script and read for the part of Norm Peterson. John saw himself in the role of Norm, the good-natured accountant who found a place to call home on a bar stool in a Boston tavern. The casting directors felt differently, however, as they chose George Wendt to play Norm Peterson.

Faced with this defining moment, Ratzenberger, quite the opposite of the man-child Cliff, who affected a blustery, boastful attitude in trying to hide his deep-seated insecurities from his friends, showed that he had a reservoir of resilient attitudes. He resisted succumbing to it's-all-over-but-the-shouting and asked the directors if the *Cheers* cast included a know-it-all bar character. To convince the directors of the value of such a character, John launched into a ten-minute, off-the-cuff monologue of useless information in the infamous style of Cliff Clavin. By fully engaging in a process he deemed as important and worthwhile to his life course, he convinced *Cheers* executives to give birth to the character of Cliff Clavin. No one gave John his good fortune; he created it on his own. He evaluated the features of the challenging stressful circumstance and seized his professional moment. The end result of his failed audition was the role of his career. He is a fine example of how being strong in all three hardy attitudes provides the courage and motivation to thrive resiliently under stress.

DENIAL AND AVOIDANCE RATHER THAN RESILIENCE

When change mounts, people who are low in the hardy attitudes feel isolated rather than committed, powerless rather than in control, and threatened rather than challenged. The resulting emotional pain leads to either of two nonresilient behavior patterns. They engage in denial and avoidance, or they panic in the face of perceived "catastrophe" and strike out.

These people deny and avoid by endorsing a rigid set of roles, rules, rituals, and relationships as the way of dealing with stressful problems. Rather than learn and grow from change, they try to fit into what others and circumstances seem to want of them. In other words, they want powerful figures to make the rules, set the pace, and tell them what to do. And, they look to long established norms, traditions, and credos to help them reject what seem like disruptive changes. All this may reduce fears and give short-term comfort and security, but it does little to open people up to new, growth-promoting situations and experiences.

Individuals who cope through denial and avoidance believe that if they stop thinking about stressful changes, the unpleasantness will go away. They believe that, when the going gets rough, it is best to withdraw or isolate to stay below radar. They resist people and circumstances that could potentially bring them pain. And, to regain peace, they detach from the stresses at hand. They won't let things upset them, trying to maintain the status quo at all costs.

These individuals view change as an irregularity, an aberration, a needless imposition. They often dwell on things that they have little influence over and avoid changes in which the outcomes are unclear. Even at home, they tend to avoid talking about work in order to preserve their sense of calm. They can lose themselves in distracting activities, such as endlessly watching TV, shopping at the mall, drinking heavily, or extrarelational flirtations, all in an effort to escape life's difficulties. You can find them saying things like, "Why try to change things? You can do very little about it anyway. I'm just doing time. Why should I care about what goes on here?"

As employees, these people often think of themselves as "company visitors," and reluctant ones at that. They do what they have to because of others' expectations, requests, and demands. Because they deny and avoid stressful changes, they engage only superficially in work tasks and don't believe that they can change or grow because of their participation. They are just doing time.

As you would imagine, these individuals are low in resiliency. They sink into feelings of powerlessness, which leave them incapable and weak. If they pull up stakes, they give up any sense of positively influencing their lives. They cherish stability and tradition, and see anything else as undermining them. Their fears of change inhibit their personal evolution and growth, as well as opportunities to enhance meaning by turning stressful changes into opportunities.

Take Vivian's story as a case in point. She was in her late thirties when the company for which she was an administrative assistant began to reorganize its product line in order to improve its market share. Soon, there were both new hires and layoffs, along with ongoing job redefinitions. All this seemed overwhelming to her, as she had always felt as if she had no influence and was vulnerable. She kept trying not to think about what was happening or listen to her coworkers' relevant discussions of the changes. She just kept doing what she regarded as her job, even though the official sense of her tasks was changing. She had nostalgic memories about previous stability, and saw the current decision makers as upstarts. Curtailing her work hours as much as possible, she spent more and more time at home watching television while drinking wine.

Before long, she was terminated, as the decision makers saw her as recalcitrant and ineffective in their company's changing times. Then, she spent even more of her time watching TV and drinking, and could not bring herself to any concerted, organized effort to find another job. She became increasingly dependent financially and emotionally on her aging parents, who were worried about her and mystified as to how to help her get back on her feet.

CATASTROPHIC REACTIONS AND STRIKING OUT, RATHER THAN BEING RESILIENT

Most of us want our coworkers and employers to recognize and value our contributions to the workplace. We have a core need for others to think well of us. Organizations often establish procedures and policies for recognizing their employees so they will stay involved, productive, and satisfied. In rapidly changing times of high workplace stress, however, these types of employee reinforcements are used less and less. It is therefore easier today to fade into the workplace woodwork, which can make employees feel insecure, powerless, and expendable.

With strong attitudes of commitment, control, and challenge, you feel secure even in unsupportive work conditions. You know how to make use of work procedures and policies to guide your work tasks and behavior. This helps you to stay motivated, despite less frequent reinforcements, and to be resilient in finding new ways to renew job interest and value.

In contrast, individuals low in the hardy attitudes are less resilient, needing more concrete guidance through well-defined work procedures and policies. There is nothing inherently bad in this, and in fact, many of these individuals make excellent supervisors and supervisees because of their appreciation of workplace procedures and policies. High stress and poorly delineated, changing circumstances, however, can leave them feeling alienated. To function effectively, they depend upon smoothly run, well-defined work environments and clearly defined work tasks and procedures for getting recognized and valued.

What is the downside to this nonresilient approach? These people overreact to changes that decrease their sense of support. Anything that disrupts routine and order is seen as a catastrophe, a sign that they are not valued and are being pushed around. Company reorganizations, shifts in management and supervisors, and ever-changing work tasks and policies make it increasingly difficult for these nonresilient individuals to pinpoint opportunities for coworkers, supervisors, and their employers to recognize and value them. They begin to classify events as nurturing or depriving, which undermines them physically, mentally, and behaviorally. By overpersonalizing workplace changes, they undermine workplace relationships. Their coworkers often avoid them in order to secure their own peace and equilibrium.

What do these more vulnerable employees really fear? They feel weak and powerless through their inability to manage change effectively. To regain mastery and control, these hardworking, self-sacrificing employees become rigid and may begin to use the measuring stick that they use on themselves to evaluate coworkers, supervisors, and employers. At such times, others may see them as critical and competitive.

There can be an extreme expression of this nonresilient coping position. Certain workplace conditions can make these individuals feel misused, injured, and wounded. Once on the defensive, they begin to view coworkers, management, and the company as adversaries. Although there may be some reality to their complaints, they channel their anxieties, fears, and floundering self-esteem through a victim mentality. Odd as it seems, this is a way for them to protect themselves when other paths close. They adopt the approach that the best defense is an offense. They recover the veneer of equilibrium and momentum by behaving contrarily.

These employees make others responsible for their stress and unhappiness. Friends, family, and coworkers avoid them, when nothing they say or do can help. These vulnerable employees are low in resilient attitudes. They have difficulty thinking about new, more adaptive ways to bolster their self-esteem, and thus they fear change. By externalizing blame, they attempt to save face. And, in the most extreme, they may cope with difficult circumstances through increased work absenteeism, poor work performance, workplace theft or vandalism, and unwarranted threats to carry out legal action against their employers.

THE IMPORTANCE OF ATTITUDES IN RESILIENCE

The two ineffective coping strategies just covered demonstrate why hardy attitudes help you face stressful problems with courage, and be resilient rather than vulnerable. To be courageous, you have to see the stressor clearly and avoid shrinking back, despite your fear of it. In addition, these attitudes motivate you, and lead you to figure out ways to turn change into opportunities and to take the necessary steps to bring about that advantage. Let's take a look at a few common situations:

- Suppose you have less job security today. Do you detach from coworkers and the company by giving a lackluster perform-ance, by cutting corners, or by being disloyal? If you have strong hardy attitudes, you sidestep these unproductive be-haviors. Instead, you cope constructively with job insecurities and accept them as today's business norm. You throw your-self into work, perform to your highest capacity, continue to learn from your experience, and treat your coworkers and employer as you like them to treat you. That's what it means to be strong in commitment, control, and challenge. After all, even if you lose your job, your ongoing diligence, conscien-tiousness, and professional development will make you all the more attractive as a prospective employee to other com-panies. And, maybe you can make your new job even better than the one you lost.

- Suppose your industry or company is such that jobs, driven by technological advance, competition, or market needs, fre-quently change in definition. Do you hang on rigidly to current ways of functioning and grow more troubled and wary over less traditional changes? If your hardy attitudes are strong, you sidestep these unproductive behaviors. You instead see such changes as opportunities to continue your development and throw yourself instead into learning and training that make sure this happens. You increase your value and marketability to your current company or another company by continuing to develop your knowledge.

■ Suppose work tasks, responsibilities, and deadlines increasingly inundate you as your company downsizes. Do you sink into resentment, detachment, and hostility? If your hardy attitudes are strong, you sidestep these unproductive behaviors. You strive instead to regroup and improve your functioning to meet the expanded requirements. If you need help in doing this, you ask constructively for assistance from your company. Before long, the company will rely on you more, and use you as a model for others. In the process, you will feel more competent and capable.

■ Suppose that with all the ongoing changes, your relationships with supervisors or subordinates in the company deteriorate through misunderstandings, arguments, and retaliations. Do you detach from others and devalue them? If your hardy attitudes are strong, you sidestep these unproductive behaviors. You try instead to understand relationship difficulties as a byproduct of stress. By encouraging and assisting others, you try to resolve workplace conflicts, rather than perpetuate them with impulsive, thoughtless actions. By valuing and helping others, and trying to improve your interactions with them, they in turn trust and value you.

WHERE DO YOU FIT IN?

When you examine your own responses to workplace changes, what do you find? How does your particular way of understanding circumstances drive your response? In which ways do you try to preserve your self-esteem during stressful circumstances? Does your pattern of response express the attitudes of commitment, control, and challenge?

Take a few minutes to think through the following questions to get a sense of how you handle stressful work changes now and in the past.

COMMITMENT, CONTROL, AND CHALLENGE

1. Do you wake up in the morning excited by the thought of going to work?

2. Despite cherishing the past, do you look forward to a changing future?

3. Do you feel that your input at work makes a difference in how things turn out?

4. Do you rely on yourself to figure out how to solve problems that arise at work?

5. Do you anticipate changes at work as bound to happen and normal?

6. Do you see both your company and yourself trying to grow and do better?

DENIAL AND AVOIDANCE

1. Do you feel most comfortable with clearly defined work tasks?

2. Do you feel most comfortable with little change in work task or environment?

3. To stay calm and happy, do you put work problems out of your mind?

4. Do you escape from work problems by distracting yourself with daydreams and other fun activities?

5. Does work stress you? If so, are you unsure as to why?

6. Do you work to pay your bills and nothing more?

CATASTROPHIC REACTIONS AND STRIKING OUT

1. At times, have you tried to undermine coworkers by devaluing their work tasks or personal characteristics in front of supervisors or management?

2. When you are part of a work team, do others' ideas and contributions threaten you?

3. Have you ever passed off as your own a coworker's ideas or work products?

4. Do you overpersonalize workplace changes?

5. Do you feel unappreciated and hurt when a supervisor highlights an area of work in which you need more growth?

6. Do you use problems outside of work to maneuver coworkers and supervisors into relieving you of work tasks?

To score your answers, give yourself one point for each time you answered "True" to a question. In order to see your attitudinal approach to stressful changes and conflicts, total your scores for each set of six questions. Which set gave you the highest score? Do you respond through hardiness, denial and avoidance, or catastrophic reactions? Then, add your total scores on denial and avoidance, and catastrophic reactions, and divide this grand total by two. Compare this number with your total score on the hardiness items, and you will see whether you respond to stressful changes with hardiness.

SUMMARY

Do you see why hardy attitudes amount to the courage and motivation to thrive in the midst of stressful changes? Now, of course, you need to supplement courage and motivation with the specific skills that will help you transform these stressful changes into opportunities. But, first, you need to deepen your resilient or hardy attitudes.

CHAPTER 6

PRACTICING YOUR ATTITUDES OF COMMITMENT, CONTROL, AND CHALLENGE

By now, you have a sense of how the attitudes of commitment, control, and challenge can help you to be resilient under stress. In this chapter, we'll explain how you can deepen your own hardy attitudes. It's always important to keep a hardy mindset, even in less stressful times. But, if stressful changes do come your way, they offer a great opportunity to test your courage and motivation to turn problems into advantage. Essentially, can you walk the talk?

STEP ONE
STUDY PEOPLE YOU KNOW WHO ARE HIGH IN RESILIENCE

Begin by thinking about people you know who are high in the attitudes of commitment, control, and challenge, and who show resilience no matter what happens to them. Remember Lou Zamperini from chapter 1? His resilience was evident, as was his courage and motivation to overcome extremely stressful circumstances. He tried to influence the outcome of whatever challenges he met in life, and did so while helping other people.

Do you know someone who is high in resilience and hardy attitudes? Whether this person's stress demands large or small efforts, does he or she stay the course, engage rather than withdraw, and grow from the experience? Use the following five key questions to analyze what this person has actually done to turn stress to advantage.

1. **WHAT STRESSFUL CIRCUMSTANCES DID HE OR SHE ENCOUNTER?** Was the stress acute (disruptive and time limited) or chronic (a mismatch between dreams, desires, and actual experience)? Remember, sometimes an acute stress stirs up chronic stresses.

2. **WHAT PROBLEM-SOLVING ACTIONS DID THE PERSON TAKE TO DECREASE THE CIRCUMSTANCES' STRESSFULNESS?** How did he or she do this? Did he or she follow up on opportunities stemming from the stressful situation?

3. **DID THE PERSON'S COPING EFFORTS INCLUDE GETTING SUPPORTIVE ASSISTANCE AND ENCOURAGEMENT FROM OTHER PEOPLE?** Did he or she reach out to others as well in this process, and if so, how?

4. **HOW DID THIS PERSON TALK ABOUT THE EXPERIENCE?** When reminiscing, observing, planning, or evaluating the stress, did the person associate the experience with his or her life direction, purpose, and meaning? Did the evaluation express new insights about circumstance, life, and self?

5. **HOW DID HIS OR HER COPING EFFORTS EXPRESS HARDY ATTITUDES?** Can you fit what he or she said or did into

commitment, control, and challenge (thought the problem was important and worthwhile enough to solve, tried to influence its outcome, and used the experience to learn and grow from)?

CASE STUDIES: PEOPLE HIGH IN RESILIENCE

The following two examples of clients we worked with can help you think about people you know with regard to resilience and hardy attitudes.

ELENA S.: "WHEN LIFE IS HARD, YOU MUST TRY EVEN HARDER."

1. What stressful circumstances did she encounter?

Elena is a marketing manager whose company was stepping up pressure on her to bring in more clients. Monthly, her anxious supervisor scrutinized her records. Under pressure himself, he was often irritable toward Elena, which amplified her stress. As if this work stress was not enough, Elena's husband wanted more of her time and attention, and her eighty-eight-year-old mother had become too frail and forgetful to live alone.

2. What did Elena do to decrease the circumstances' stressfulness?

In what follows, you will see that Elena faced the realities of these stressful circumstances, despite their painfulness. She had little time for personal enjoyment, like reading. As much as this disappointed her, she had priorities that demanded attention. Elena sufficiently tended to her work and home pressures, and when plagued by doubt, panic, or anger, she tried hard to counter these reactions through solutions that serviced her best interests. So, each time she had a stressful interaction with her boss or husband, she reflected upon it, hoping to gain insight into what was going on, and then tried to communicate better or unilaterally suggest plans that would help.

3. Did Elena's coping efforts include getting supportive assistance and encouragement from other people?

Despite her boss's irritability, Elena set up meetings with him to discuss ways in which they could build their client base. She resisted personalizing his frustrations, despite her own stress. Sometimes her boss opened up and talked about company troubles. With sincere interest, Elena listened to him and asked how she could help. This seemed to clear tensions between them so that their strategizing meetings became more productive. In a better economy, the marketing department relied on long-standing clients who, year to year, gave them a tremendous amount of business. It was easier in those days to escape the attention of upper management, because more-than-adequate quotas kept the marketing department below radar. At the end of the twentieth century, however, many of their stable clients went belly-up. No longer able to rest on their laurels, they developed a plan to open up new markets. Elena needed support from her boss to begin the problem-solving process, and it seemed like he needed the same of her.

4. How did Elena talk about the experience? Did the evaluation express new insights about circumstance, life, and self?

Elena realized that she had initially responded to stresses by lapsing into a work routine that sapped her creativity and energy. She began to act more like an account manager than like a market strategist. Through her company's dissatisfaction with her department's performance, she realized she was in a professional and personal slump. She also realized how much she missed social interactions with friends, family, and coworkers, and how insufficient social opportunities contributed to her stress.

By putting her work life into perspective, Elena was freer to focus on bettering her home life. This stressed her much less, although there were still work changes to deal with. She could pay more attention to loved ones, which her husband enjoyed, because she now had energy. He agreed with Elena that her mother should live with them and vowed willingly to help make this transition successful. Even though her mother now required assistance, Elena wanted to do everything she could to assure her mother's independence. To do this, Elena and her husband planned to give Elena's mother manageable chores to maintain her mental and emotional functioning.

5. How did Elena's coping efforts express the attitudes of commitment, control, and challenge?

Elena is high in hardy attitudes. She dealt actively with job and work pressures. Instead of running away, she sought the help of others, built rather than tore down bridges, and faced personal limitations that added to her stress. Along with this, she disallowed negative preoccupations and instead focused on assisting her boss. Elena clearly sees her life as important and worthwhile enough to engage in fully (commitment rather than isolation). She put energy into healing relationships and developing plans to increase the marketing department's client base (control rather than powerlessness). And, she seized personally beneficial opportunities to grow in the stressful work change (challenge rather than threat).

HERMAN W.: "THERE'S A SILVER LINING IN EVERY CLOUD, IF YOU CARE TO FIND IT."

1. What stressful circumstance did he encounter?

Herman slowly moved up the ranks at his company. He worked as a manager in the human resources department for several of the twenty-five years of his employment. His company abruptly notified him that they were eliminating his department because of the need to downsize personnel and decentralize company functions. The long and short of it is that Herman no longer had a job. This news sideswiped and upset him, especially since it was a financially inopportune time for this to happen to his family. Herman's wife planned to retire when their children started college next year. Now, more than ever, they needed his income.

2. What did Herman do to decrease the circumstance's stressfulness?

At first, Herman felt victimized and angry at the system. "How could the people I've worked with and trusted for twenty years just call me in and tell me I don't have a job anymore?" He worried whether he was too old to get another job of similar rank and income. When the initial shock faded, Herman began to think things through more calmly.

Rather than continue to imagine the worst about his long-time colleagues, he approached them with questions and listened to what they had to say. He came to recognize that, as operating costs soared and revenues declined, the company needed to mollify investors by streamlining in any way that it could. Like many companies today, his company was beginning to outsource human resource functions. It was the department rather than Herman, they said, that was dispensable. It hurt, but Herman knew this was a sign of the times.

3. Did Herman's coping efforts include getting supportive assistance and encouragement from other people?

Herman knew his age, salary, and experience might work against him in the job marketplace. He loved his work and did not want to start at square one again. Herman calmly began thinking. He knew other companies would soon outsource their human resource functions too, if they had not done so already. Throughout the years, he formed good collegial relationships with his coworkers, management, and customers. It occurred to him that his years of expertise and success in this field would make him a valued human resources consultant. To move forward with this plan, he ran this idea by his former colleagues. They became Herman's first client, which also lessened their guilt of having to let him go. Herman had just enough income from this initial client to cover the costs of starting his consulting company.

4. How did Herman talk about the experience? Did his evaluation express new insights about circumstance, life, and self?

Several successful years later, Herman was happier than ever. This new chapter in his life, he thought, was possible because of the stressful work change. He's never bored and makes more money than before. And, according to Herman, this opportunity added purpose and meaning to his life. His wife really came through for him too. She helped him pick up the pieces by working part-time with him. They had not collaborated like this for years and enjoyed the meaningful connection. Herman's children started college, and they are doing quite well.

Even though it was stressful at the time, Herman sees leaving the company more positively now. He had the insight that the company disliked the push to evolve as much as he did. "By outsourcing human resource functions, they found a way to cope with change. I know it sounds simple, but until now, I lacked awareness of how closely their fears and tasks matched mine. It's hard sometimes to see the big picture, especially when you're hurting." Herman has a greater sense now of the impersonal disposition of outside forces. Although he saw others come and go throughout the years, he expected to survive. Today, Herman appreciates the laws of change. "Although I will always try to positively influence what happens to me, I'll blame others less for doing what they have to do."

5. How did Herman's coping efforts express the attitudes of commitment, control, and challenge?

Once Herman's shock wore off, he sought out his colleagues to understand what happened. He further convinced his company to be his first client. And, his coping efforts extended to his wife. Herman found a way for her to retire by working with him in the new business. His commitment, control, and challenge are quite clear.

STRENGTHENING YOUR HARDY ATTITUDES

Can you think of a stressful change or circumstance when *you* showed hardy attitudes? Whether the stress demanded a large or small effort, did you stay on course, engage rather than withdraw, and grow from the experience when the going got rough? At the risk of repeating ourselves in order to emphasize their importance, use the five key questions to think through what you actually did to turn stress to your advantage.

1. What stressful circumstance did you encounter? Was the stress acute or chronic? Remember, sometimes an acute stress stirs up chronic stress.

2. What actions did you take to decrease the circumstance's stressfulness? How did you do this? Did you follow up on opportunities stemming from the stressful situation? What did you do?

3. Did your coping efforts include getting supportive assistance and encouragement from other people? Did you reach out to others as well in this process, and if so, how?

4. How did you talk about the experience? When reminiscing, observing, planning, or evaluating the stress, did you associate the experience with your life direction, purpose, and meaning? Did the evaluation express new insights about circumstance, life, and self?

5. How did your coping efforts express hardy attitudes? Can you fit what you said or did into commitment, control, and challenge? Finally, imagine your future. How do strong attitudes of commitment, control, and challenge make a difference in your experience and events? As you go through daily stress, see if your hardy attitudes make a difference in how you experience it.

STEP TWO
BE AWARE OF THE DISADVANTAGES OF ISOLATION, POWERLESSNESS, AND THREAT

Another aspect of thinking in a resilient way is to maintain a keen awareness of the long-term disadvantages of withdrawing (rather than staying committed), sinking into powerlessness (rather than exerting an influence), and searching for easy comfort and security (rather than continuing to learn through change). Think of people you know who let stressful changes undermine them because they fail to be hardy under pressure. If you think through what they do compared to those who cope resiliently, you get a clear sense of the differences, and you can refer to this the next time a stressful change happens to you.

PEOPLE YOU KNOW WHO ARE LOW IN RESILIENCE

Make a list of the people you know who seem deficient in hardy attitudes, people who withdraw and feel powerless and threatened. Write down each of their stories. In this regard, it will be helpful for you to answer the same five key questions about them:

1. What stressful circumstance did he or she encounter?

2. What actions did the person take to decrease the circumstance's stressfulness? Did he or she follow up on opportunities stemming from the stressful situation?

3. Did the person's coping efforts include getting supportive assistance and encouragement from other people?

4. How did this person talk about the experience?

5. How did his or her coping efforts express hardy attitudes or the lack of commitment, control, and challenge?

CASE STUDIES: PEOPLE LOW IN RESILIENCE

Here are three real-life examples of unfortunate people deficient in hardy attitudes. Mulling over their lives may help you recognize precisely how the disadvantages of nonresilient or low-resilient attitudes overwhelmed them as they encountered daily life experiences:

ALLAN H.: "LIFE STINKS, AND THERE'S NOTHING I CAN DO ABOUT IT."

1. What stressful circumstance did Allan encounter?

Allan grew up in a comfortable, upper-middle-class neighborhood. His parents overprotected him; they grew up poor, prospered, and desired to give Allan everything they had not had. He played soccer throughout middle school, and in high school, he was on the track team. In college, Allan spent more time socializing than studying, which most likely contributed to his average academic performance. Soon after graduating, he married, and shortly thereafter, he and his wife started a family. They have two daughters.

Allan parlayed his college computer training into a job with a high-tech company as a software writer. He made a very good income with stock options. Allan had found his life's work, which delighted him. It pleased him that his family was much better off financially than other people he knew.

From time to time, Allan heard office rumors that the company he worked for had been over-reporting its earnings. Allan never took this too seriously; he trusted his employer and the financial stability of the company. Before he realized it, his company's stock plummeted in value. Allan lost his job, his health benefits, and had little financial assets to speak of. This dismayed his wife, a stay-at-home mom; Allan felt like a failure. It did not help that his children could not understand this reversal of fortune either, as they had always looked up to their father.

2. What actions did Allan take to decrease the circumstance's stressfulness?

Allan had difficulty getting over what happened and kept seeing himself as the victim of others who were just jealous of him. He withdrew from everyone, sat at home watching television, and began drinking heavily. He made one or two half-hearted efforts to find another job, but he lacked sufficient energy to make this happen. Allan convinced himself those other companies too would use and take advantage of him. He tearfully reminisced about his happy childhood, when people were trustworthy. As evidenced by his company's deceit, Allan disbelieved in people's genuineness and worried about the world's deteriorating condition.

3. Did Allan get supportive assistance and encouragement during this stressful time?

Before long, Allan became deeply bitter, distrustful, and self-pitying. He lacked energy and imagination to find solutions to his problems, which lowered his self-esteem. Eventually, a whole series of life reversals ensued. His mortgage went unpaid, and the family lost its sumptuous home. Allan's desperate wife was unsuccessful in talking with him. His neediness exhausted her, and he refused to get help. To survive, she left, taking the kids with her. He was furious because she rejected him in his time of need. Allan's use of alcohol to medicate his pain resulted in a driving-under-the-influence charge. As time went on, Allan failed to turn his life around.

4. How did Allan talk about the experience? When reminiscing, observing, planning, or evaluating the stress, did he associate the experience with his life direction, purpose, and meaning? Did the evaluation express new insights about circumstance, life, and self?

Allan expressed his plight with bitterness about the world around him, and lots of self-pity. From his viewpoint, people either do not care at all about others, or are actually vicious. Organizations and social institutions were also described by him as bent on undermining the people within them, despite official presentations to the contrary. He was also preoccupied by the injustices piled on him, and how this victimization had destroyed his life. He would often cry when reflecting on these painful conclusions.

5. How did his coping efforts express hardy attitudes or the lack of commitment, control, and challenge?

Note that Allan's lack of hardy attitudes prevented him from making resilient use of the experience. He withdrew from rather than committing to the events and people around him, and sank into powerlessness, anger, and passivity when the going got rough. To him, you avoid threatening changes rather than use them as an impetus for learning and growth.

GRACE H.: "THIS IS A MALE SOCIETY, AND I'M UNFORTUNATELY A WOMAN."

Grace hoped to move up the company ranks in a small clothing firm that specialized in designing and producing women's clothing. As an administrative assistant, she followed company procedures and policies by the book. Grace gave the company 110 percent of herself. She rarely complained, if at all, and valued responsible action.

She had grown up in a poor family, and it had always been an effort to go to school and work part-time simultaneously. After dropping out of college, she found her present job and threw herself into it.

As the years went by, the company passed Grace by for promotions. She noticed that younger, junior men tended to rise up in the company. This particularly irritated her, as she had trained them in their jobs. Once, while talking with her boss, she summoned up the courage to ask him about this situation. He superficially responded, claiming that those who the company promotes possess particular capabilities. "If, you wait," he stated, "your time will come." This proved to be untrue.

She did not bring the matter up again for fear that retribution would follow. Grace's personal insecurities stopped her from looking for another job. She told herself, "I need the money," so she stayed put. Over time, Grace lost her self-esteem. She carelessly carried out work tasks and gave very little of herself to her job and coworkers. She kept to herself. She felt stuck in a thankless job; this depressed her. Grace gained weight, slipped into poor grooming habits, and, to avoid pain, she watched television endlessly, overspent at the mall, and occasionally got drunk.

Grace felt her father favored her brothers over her. She believed her boss did the same thing to her. She expressed more and more anger toward men and a patriarchal society, which, she felt, conspired to put women down. Even though she could get angry when forced to think about her difficulties, she preferred to avoid it all and lose herself in distracting activities. "Why waste my time putting emotion and energy into this problem," she stated, "this is the way the world works; it's less painful to accept my life as it is today."

You can see Grace lacks the hardy attitudes to be resilient. When there are problems, she avoids them and just gives up trying. She suppresses angry feelings by losing herself in self-destructive activities. Although it may be true that some companies advance more men over women, she uses her views as a blanket justification for giving up rather than as an observation that could lead to corrective efforts. Grace will have trouble turning disadvantages into opportunities, unless her attitudes change considerably.

MARTIN O.: "JUST KEEP BEING OPTIMISTIC; THINGS WILL TURN OUT FOR THE BEST."

Martin had similar beginnings to Allan. He grew up in an upper-middle-class family. His father, who grew up poor, wanted Martin to have every opportunity to make it in life. He made everyday life comfortable for Martin. Martin never struggled. Although he got through college, he did so uneventfully. He performed poorly. He referred to his average grades as "gentlemanly Cs." Martin had no experience with adversity. He felt optimistic about his future, even though he had no big plans or goals in mind. He was handsome, had many friends, played sports, and dated many girls. Martin showed little concern that life might turn out poorly for him.

Upon graduating with a major in business, many companies offered Martin jobs. He took a job in sales, which seemed right to him because he always enjoyed meeting and talking with people. In job training, he superficially learned about company products and strategies for selling them. Martin relied on his charm and social skills to engage potential customers. Before long, while other sales representatives increased their customer base, Martin had little to show for his efforts. His supervisor showed more concern over Martin's performance than Martin did. The supervisor talked to Martin about it and encouraged him to try harder. Martin took lightly his supervisor's concerns and continued in his ways. He occasionally sold a customer. Nevertheless, his selling efforts failed more than succeeded. It pleased him to bring in a new customer, though it was a rare occurrence.

Soon, his company terminated him because of his poor performance. Martin saw his termination as a temporary setback, and optimistically maintained that everything would work out in the end. Martin presented well. He easily got another sales job, and his social skills always got him through customers' doors, but his reluctance to give up unproductive work behaviors prevented him from making sales. Here, too, his performance was lackluster. This company also terminated him for poor performance and lack of motivation to improve. Once again, Martin had little insight as to why the company terminated him. This pattern continued over the years.

Martin's deficiency in hardy attitudes is more subtle than either Allan's or Grace's. His optimism at first may appear hardy, but superficial buoyancy can be a way of denying and avoiding problems. It's difficult to solve problems you fail to see. Martin's cheerful ways and social interest makes him seem committed to influence life circumstances. But, Martin's naive optimism did him in. If you think changes and problems always turn out well without your effort, why put energy or time into working constructively to transform them? Naive optimism prevented Martin from seeing how life's changes, positive or negative, can be opportunities to learn and grow. His laissez-faire approach to life hurt him in the end.

AVOID VULNERABLE ATTITUDES

By now, you are probably very alert to the disadvantages of responding to stressful circumstances with the vulnerable attitudes of withdrawal, powerlessness, and threat. You need to keep in mind how these attitudes in the people you know, and in the examples we have reported, undermined the process of turning stress to advantage through involvement, influential effort, and attempts to keep learning.

Now it is time for you to observe yourself as honestly as you can to see if and when you have sunken into attitudes of withdrawal (rather than commitment), powerlessness (rather than control), and threat (rather than challenge).

Looking back: Think about your past.

- Do you remember concrete examples or extended periods of time when you avoided or reacted catastrophically to changes that were disruptive and stressful?

- Did you try to avoid the disruptive changes?

- Did you get angry enough to strike out?

- Did you give up trying?

- Did you come to the conclusion that life just isn't fair?

Try to see behind these actions the nonresilient attitudes of withdrawal, powerlessness, and threat. Make yourself a list of the troublesome events and your disadvantageous reactions to them.

Looking at today: Now make an honest appraisal of the present.

- Are there concrete examples or extended periods of time when you have failed to express the attitudes of commitment, control, and challenge?

- What are the particular characteristics of the stressful circumstances that have this effect on you?

- Is your inclination to withdraw, sink into powerlessness, and find changes too threatening to learn from?

- Do you justify it to yourself with pessimistic conclusions as to what life is all about?

Write down your observations concerning your present-day functioning.

Looking ahead: How about your future? When you think of the days, months, and years ahead:

- Do you hope that nothing will change and lack an elaborate plan as to what your life will become?

- Do you think the world will get worse, rather than get better, and that there is nothing any of us can do about that?

- Or, do you look forward to the meaningful evolution of society, the world, and yourself?

Even if you have found signs that you can sink into withdrawal, powerlessness, and threat, don't give up. Identifying these attitudinal problems is an important step toward getting rid of them. Remember how troubled the lives are of the people you know who are nonresilient and the examples we have given you here in Step Two, and resolve not to let this happen to you. Instead, focus on the resilient people you know and the examples discussed in Step One. Try to follow in their footsteps of commitment, control, and challenge, and you will truly be able to say, "Whatever doesn't kill me makes me stronger."

STEP THREE
HOW YOU FEEL ABOUT YOURSELF WHEN YOU TURN STRESSFUL CHANGES TO ADVANTAGE

So far, we have tried to get you to immerse yourself in what happens concerning resilience when you have or don't have hardy attitudes. Whatever your present attitudinal inclination, you are trying to keep in mind the advantages of commitment, control, and challenge, and the disadvantages of withdrawal, powerlessness, and threat. As you involve yourself more and more in this process, it should have a beneficial effect on you.

There is yet a third way to increase your hardy attitudes. Of the three steps discussed here, it is the most powerful. It involves expressing the resiliency skills needed to turn disruptive, stressful changes from potential disasters into opportunities, and using the feedback you get from your efforts to convince yourself that you can make a meaningful difference in how your life unfolds and improves. In other words, you will have the courage to do what helps, and develop in the process. Chapters 7, 8, 9, and 10 deal with exercising the skills of transformational coping and social support. In transformational coping, you think of stressful changes as problems to be solved and take the necessary steps to achieve that end. When it comes to support, you arrange to give and get assistance and encouragement from those around you, so that you all can believe in yourselves and carry out the hard work of problem solving. In the process of employing both coping and support skills, you get feedback from your efforts.

THREE SOURCES OF FEEDBACK

The *first source of feedback* comes from the observations you make of yourself as you engage in your efforts. The coping exercises in chapters 7 and 8 guide you in how to structure stressful changes as problems, and how to go about turning them to advantage. As you observe yourself carrying out these exercises, you may well think, "Is that me? I didn't know I could do that." The social support exercises in chapters 9 and 10 guide you in resolving conflicts with the significant people around you, and replacing those conflicts with a mutual pattern of assistance and encouragement. As you observe yourself carrying out these exercises, you may well think, "I didn't know how constructively I could interact with those people. It's great that I was able to strengthen my relationships with them."

How does feedback from observing yourself in action benefit you? By seeing yourself cope and interact constructively, you strengthen your hardy attitudes of commitment, control, and challenge.

The *second source of feedback* is the observations that others make of you and tell you about. When you use the right skills to cope and interact, people will note the changes in you and may well communicate what they see. Or, you may ask them for their observations. Typically, they will admire the changes you are making toward greater incisiveness and constructive involvement. They may tell you about this directly, in such words as, "I respect what you have done so much. To tell you the truth, I didn't think it was possible." At worst, they may express jealousy toward you. But, behind this, of course, is envious admiration.

How does feedback from others who observe you in action benefit you? Their comments motivate you to cope constructively again, reinforce your learning, and deepen your connection to them. This type of feedback deepens your attitudes of commitment, control, and challenge.

The *third source of feedback* is the actual effect your actions have on the target events and/or people. Your actions that come out of the training exercises aim at turning potential disasters to advantage and deepening the intimacy of your relationships with those around you. As you begin to achieve these goals, you get concrete signs of how your life is improving, both in and out of the workplace. This feedback, too, will convince you more and more that it is worth involving yourself (commitment), trying to have an effect (control), and learning through the changes (challenge), rather than withdrawing and feeling powerless and threatened.

SUMMARY

We hope you can see even more clearly now why hardy attitudes provide you with the courage and motivation to work resiliently at improving your own situation and the lives of those around you. It takes courage to see change as natural, despite its stressfulness, and as an opportunity to grow and develop to your fullest at work and at home. To strengthen your hardy attitudes, keep practicing the exercises covered in the first two steps of this chapter. In this regard, remember to:

- Keep reflecting on people you know who are strong in hardy attitudes and resiliency.

- Keep reflecting on the disadvantages of feeling isolated, powerless, and threatened.

- Apply this to your own beliefs as you struggle for the resilience to turn stressful circumstances to advantage.

Further, to really deepen your attitudes of commitment, control, and challenge, engage fully in the coping and social support exercises of chapters 7, 8, 9, and 10, conscientiously using the feedback you get from your efforts to influence how you think of yourself, your job, and your life.

CHAPTER 7

TRANSFORMATIONAL COPING: TURNING STRESSFUL CHANGES TO YOUR ADVANTAGE

"The significant problems we face cannot be solved at the same level of thinking we were at when we created them."

—ALBERT EINSTEIN[1]

You have a choice as to the way in which you cope with stressful changes. The way of transformational, or resilient, coping is to:

- Treat changes as problems to solve,

- Take the necessary mental and action steps to solve problems effectively, and

- Draw observations, insights, and wisdom from your coping experiences in order to learn and grow.

Each time you cope in this way, you make yourself better prepared for the next problem as it arises.

Specifically, at the mental level, you find a way to put the stressful circumstance into a broader perspective, so that it seems less daunting. Then, you are able to analyze the circumstance's subtle features and deepen your understanding of it. The mental steps of broadening perspective and deepening understanding lead you toward an action plan that can decrease the stress and turn the change to your advantage. Carrying out the action plan can increase your hardy attitudes, which increases the likelihood that you will continue with transformational coping as other changes happen.

TRANSFORMATIONAL COPING

"In the middle of every difficulty lies opportunity."
—ALBERT EINSTEIN[2]

Transformational coping is a proactive mental and behavioral coping style that is fundamental to resiliency. Through coping in this way, the negative emotions around stressful problems diminish, and new ways of thinking open pathways for effective action. With this process, stressful changes can be turned into opportunities. But, to turn adversity to your advantage, you must put effort into finding new ways of understanding your problems in order to arrive at new solutions. This effort is difficult; that's why, to some, it is easier to rely on old ways of understanding, as if there were nothing more to learn. When minor changes are experienced, this status-quo approach may be all you need to cope. But, when stressful changes require new understanding and coping behaviors to solve them, the status-quo approach amounts to coping regressively. Old ways of understanding problems often spotlight a stressful change's obvious features rather than its subtle ones, which obscure pathways to solving the problem.

Transformational coping's procedures and skills help you to

uncover the subtle features of stressful change. When you sort out the possibilities of a circumstance, you have a chance to turn change to advantage, grow in understanding, and make headway in carving a professional and personal path that moves you positively into the future.

To get you started, let's look at the three key steps in transformational coping:

1. **BROADENING YOUR PERSPECTIVE.** The transformational coping process begins at the mental level. Many of the stressful work changes you face today happen at an organizational level, despite that they affect you personally. It helps to solve these large-scale difficulties by placing them into a broader perspective so that they are more tolerable. You can then back up enough to get a bird's-eye view of these problems, so you can think about them clearly and decide how to cope with them.

For example, you might put a job loss into perspective by realizing that internal and external conditions had reached a point where the company felt that downsizing was necessary to get back on track. And, of course, downsizing leads employers to terminate employees, not an act of personal aggression against you. You can now think through the pros and cons of the job loss and come up with a constructive plan of action. When you make the stressor tolerable by broadening your perspective, you are more ready and able to analyze the problem and search out a solution to it.

2. **DEEPENING YOUR UNDERSTANDING.** Once you gain perspective and can face the problem, you immerse yourself in the problem-solving process by taking account of the ways in which you, others, and the situation contribute to the stressfulness of the circumstance. You try to understand the less obvious features of the problem. One way to do this is by appreciating the relational facets of stressful changes.

You, and your problems, coexist with other people. For example, you and your supervisor may not get along, but because the work situation imposes upon you a collegial partnership, you must find a way to work well together. It helps little to chalk up your mutually shared uneasiness to having come from different worlds and letting it go at that. This is a regressive coping conclusion that gives you little reason to deepen your understanding of this stressful relationship.

In contrast, the transformational coping process helps you to get the most out of stressful circumstances and changes, so that you seize opportunities that lead to insights and behaviors that positively service your life. By carefully analyzing the relational facets of stressful circumstances, hardy problem solvers are able to flush outgrowth-promoting opportunities.

In the example used above, if you really analyze the difficulty you and your supervisor are having in working together, you may well be able to discern specific misunderstandings between you, and how they tend to accumulate without either of you realizing it. This will much more likely lead you to an action plan for correcting the problem than would the simple conclusion that you two just come from different worlds.

3. TAKING DECISIVE ACTION.

> *"Opportunity is missed by most because it is dressed in*
> *overalls and looks like work."*
> —THOMAS J. EDISON[3]

Gaining insight into what stresses you is good, but taking decisive action to solve the problem is even better. Once you gain perspective and understanding through the mental part of the coping process, the next step is to map out a strategy for turning around the circumstance and decreasing its stressfulness on you. Continuing with the above example, if, for instance, you concluded that a series of mutual misunderstandings caused the problem, you can take actions to clarify both your understanding of it and your supervisor's understanding of it. Your action plan might involve ways for you to explain yourself more clearly to your supervisor, and to ask for further clarification of his or her input.

The result may well be a decrease in the stressfulness of the circumstance, and the personal feedback you get from seeing yourself solving problems in this way strengthens your hardy attitudes of commitment, control, and challenge. You will increasingly feel like staying involved in your life, trying to influence the outcomes going on around you, and continually learning from your experiences, so as to do better and better.

CASE STUDIES OF TRANSFORMATIONAL COPING

The following two examples of employees skilled in transformational coping involve the mental process of putting the stressful circumstance into perspective, deepening your understanding of it, and formulating and carrying out a plan of action designed to turn things to your advantage.

JOEY T.: "HOWEVER INVOLVED IN MY WORK I AM, I CANNOT JUST DETACH FROM MY COWORKERS."

Ever since his own high school experience, Joey had wanted to be teach youngsters. After college, he started working as a math teacher in his local high school, and threw himself into making a difference in the lives of his students. Soon, he became a really popular teacher, and students treated him as one of them.

In his dedication to teaching, Joey made little effort to get to know his fellow teachers. Sometimes, he would not even go to faculty meetings, as he felt preoccupied by the effortful, time-consuming commitment to helping youngsters develop. It surprised him when he became an object of criticism for his colleagues. Even the school principal began to question Joey's intentions and effectiveness as a teacher. There was a chance that he might be officially reprimanded for being too involved with students.

Although the criticism surprised Joey, his hardy attitudes were strong enough to provoke the needed attention to his colleagues. He put the problem in perspective by recognizing that it was manageable, and could be solved. Thinking the situation through analytically, he recognized that it was his not having treated the other teachers as important that had caused the problem. He had been too exclusively occupied with helping his students.

His ensuing action plan set the goal of explaining himself to colleagues, and drawing them into his dedicated approach to reaching and influencing youngsters. He made sure never to miss faculty meetings again, and went out of his way to interact with coworkers, making sure they knew what he was trying to accomplish, and asking them about their own plans.

Before long, the majority of his colleagues began to understand and respect him as someone who was actually able to reach youngsters while teaching them. His principal asked him to carry out teaching workshops for the faculty. Joey did this with affection and humility, and before long he was influential in helping his colleagues to develop as teachers. In all this, he realized that he had been too one-sided as to the people he should reach.

RUTH B.: "WHATEVER HAPPENS, I NEED TO MAKE IT TURN OUT THE BEST FOR ME."

Pursuing an English major in college, Ruth had always wanted to be a writer. After getting her bachelor's degree, she found a job as an assistant at a large advertising firm. Her supervisor conceptualized advertising scenarios, writing a lot of them himself. He expected Ruth to carry out his plans, edit his scripts, and follow his directions.

The advertising firm had essentially one huge client. The client paid so well and needed so much marketing that, over time, the advertising firm had given up other smaller clients and concentrated efforts on the one account. Picture what this meant when, in a time of economic recession, the client had to decrease its advertising budget. When the advertising firm had to downsize as a result, Ruth, who was, after all, a junior employee, lost her job.

At first, Ruth was bewildered. She had been making a good salary. What was she to do now? Did she fail to convince them of her value as an employee? Soon, however, her hardy attitudes kicked in. She had falsely assumed that her company was solid and impervious to change, which in the past had made her feel safe. Realizing this, she recognized that she hadn't failed the company, the company had failed her and itself by putting all its eggs in one basket. She remembered that she had taken orders rather than giving them. And come to think of it, her work tasks had bored her, as they rarely expressed her talents and capabilities.

Ruth's thinking led to the perspective she reached, namely, that it is normal to shop around for jobs until you find the one that really works for you, and that it makes sense, too. Although her firm had gotten rid of her, losing her job may have been as much an opportunity as a loss. Thus, Ruth felt better and was able to analyze her situation more deeply and realize that she needed to find another job that encouraged and valued her talents more than the one she had lost.

Soon, she had an action plan and was carrying it out by applying to other advertising firms, making sure that the job they might offer would permit her to express her capabilities, and that the prospective employer knew her talents.

Before long, Ruth found what she wanted. A small firm searching for people who write well offered her a creative job. She enthusiastically accepted their offer. She's doing very well in her new job. Her coworkers respect and value her work, and she values them as colleagues and mentors. She also fully realizes that if she had not been terminated by her last employer, the new career opportunity might never have happened.

REGRESSIVE COPING

"A life spent making mistakes is not only more honorable but more useful than a life spent in doing nothing."
—GEORGE BERNARD SHAW[4]

A much less effective coping style than transformational coping is *regressive coping*. There are two expressions to this nonresilient coping style. In the first, most passive form of regressive coping, problems that stem from stressful changes are not thought about. Instead they are avoided by engaging in activities irrelevant to the task. Although this approach may bring some momentary relief, it does little to remedy the problems. Over time, individuals who take this approach learn to avoid any change that might expose their limitations and areas of needed growth. To avoid feeling awkward, out of control, and insecure, they would rather shrink their life down to the size of a postage stamp.

Exaggeration of, and catastrophic reactions to, stressful changes is the second, more active form of regressive coping. Here, you feel like a victim and strike out against those who seem like oppressors. People who cope in this way have a difficult time distinguishing between type and intensity of stressor. They respond to a change or problem that makes them feel out of control with apprehension, fear, and anger. This can manifest as irritability, uncooperativeness, and criticism of others. The more socially destructive form of this regressive coping can involve violence and acting out, such as in sabotage or terrorism. Though they differ in terms of social impact, both of these forms of regressive coping limit your effectiveness and development.

CASE STUDIES OF REGRESSIVE COPING

The five people in the following examples used different kinds of regressive coping to manage stressful changes. This coping strategy undermined their ability to develop a broad perspective and deep understanding of the problem, and to take actions that give purpose and meaning to their professional and personal lives. These five examples illustrate how bitterness and self-pity prevent people from moving forward constructively.

ALLAN H.: "LIFE STINKS, AND THERE'S NOTHING I CAN DO ABOUT IT."

The story of Allan that appeared in chapter 6 is a good example of regressive coping. Lacking courage and motivation, he was unable to do the hard work of transformational coping and slipped further and further into regressive coping instead. Because he was unable to establish himself in what he saw as a hostile world, his financial situation worsened. He could not bear to make his lifestyle more modest and hated all those fellow employees whom he saw as having done him in. He felt like such a failure. Before long, he fulfilled his prophesy through excessive drinking and drug use, so that he could feel better about himself and not think about what was happening to him.

His wife finally left their marriage, which bewildered and emotionally hurt him. While driving under the influence, he hit a teenage pedestrian, which led to his arrest and hospital-based rehabilitation. Nothing seemed to help him. When last heard from, Allan was unemployed, homeless, and down-and-out. As Allan's example shows, regressive coping becomes a nightmare syndrome, even when at first it may seem like a natural enough way of avoiding pressures. Stressed out, we may think, "What's so bad about having a few drinks or spending all my money at the mall if it helps me to distract myself from all this trouble?" Remember, one thing in regressive coping leads to another, and another, until before long, you have unwittingly undermined your life.

The answer to dealing with stressful changes in the workplace is transformational coping, because it helps you solve problems. Imagine how Allan's situation would turn out if he coped in this way:

At the mental level, he would have put losing his job in a broader perspective, making it tolerable. He could have done this by seeing his job loss as the same thing that is happening to lots of other employees like him rather than as a sign that he is just no good. This *commonplace perspective* highlights shared aspects of stressful changes. Through this, Allan could have recognized that the frequent job changes prevalent in his industry means that, though losing your position is disruptive, it hardly stops you from getting another job, perhaps an even better one with another firm. We call this the *manageability perspective.*

Had Allan approached his stressful circumstance from these perspectives, he could have assuaged his worries long enough to understand his situation more thoroughly.

- What, specifically, did the company tell him about his job loss?

- How might it be willing to help him find another placement?

- What severance benefits could he negotiate from the company?

- How could he get helpful directions by networking with his colleagues, friends, and former customers?

- Considering his assets, how much time did he have to find another position?

- What other ways are available to him in searching for other jobs?

- Is there some other job description or career he had thought of as attractive, or always wanted, for which this forced change could open the way?

By asking these questions of himself, Allan could have broadened his perspective and deepened his understanding of his situation. This would also have prepared him to develop a decisive action plan and carry it out.

Notice that we would not have wanted him to jump into an action plan without making the mental effort necessary to guide it well. The impulsive ready-fire-aim approach does more harm than good. Decisive plans for action include a goal to reach and instrumental steps toward achieving it. This all follows from a thorough understanding of the problem. Then, it would have been time for Allan to start taking the steps of his action plan, in the specified order, to reach the goal that seemed best for him. As he took the steps and reached the goal, that would have encouraged him to use the feedback from his efforts to deepen his hardy attitudes of commitment, control, and challenge. All this would have led him far from bitterness and self-pity.

GRACE H.: "THIS IS A MALE SOCIETY, AND I'M UNFORTUNATELY A WOMAN."

Now recall Grace, the example in chapter 6 of an employee low in hardy attitudes. Not surprisingly, she had sunk into bitterness, regarding herself a powerless woman in a man's world, and into self-pity that jeopardized any effort on her own behalf. This all came about when her company failed to promote her. She worked hard on work tasks, finished them as soon as possible, and geared up for the next work project. Grace contributed a lot of effort, time, and expertise to the company at which she worked. In her view, she was a model employee and, as she built up tenure, had fully expected the company to promote her. It never crossed her mind that she approached the job as a follower rather than as a leader, or that leaders are more likely to get promoted than followers.

Instead, she externalized blame, concluding that her male boss dismissed her as her father had done, and she could do little about this. It was quite painful for her to grow up with two brothers whom her father favored. Her father regularly supported his sons as the ones who would have productive careers. In contrast, he expected Grace to marry and have children. She felt her father overlooked her school success; something he never did with her brothers. Grace's father, himself not having finished high school, was traditional and had little appreciation as to why she wanted to go to college. Without the support and guidance of family members, she did poorly in school, and, after only two years, decided to drop out to get a job with her present employer. To this day, her father cannot understand why she has not married and become a mother.

To find a way to feel competent and valuable, she threw herself into her work, giving it all her energy. She assumed that the rest of the world did not share in her father's antiquated views of women in general, and of her specifically. The initial welcoming attitude of her boss led Grace to think she had finally found a place that valued her. If she followed orders and worked hard, she assumed she would rise up in the company. So, the only way that she could understand her coworkers being promoted over her was to conclude that her boss held the same male chauvinistic views as her father. She angrily decided that they were both male chauvinists. Grace knew too well this long-standing, chronic stress. She would have suffered less and found a more constructive understanding of her lack of advancement within the company if she could have embraced Eleanor Roosevelt's wise saying, "No one can make you feel inferior without your consent."

As time went on, Grace continued to cope regressively, which deepened bitter and self-piteous feelings within her. Fortunately, her church made our hardiness-training program available to its parishioners. The transformational coping part of this training program put her through exercises, like those in chapter 8. Through this, she searched for perspective and understanding of her circumstance, which led to a decisive plan of action that could solve her problem. It was hard for her to get going at first because she was so used to coping regressively. Once she involved herself in the exercises, however, and experienced some relief from coping constructively, her problem-solving process took on a life of its own. We will talk about Grace's progress in the next chapter.

MARTIN O.: "JUST KEEP BEING OPTIMISTIC; THINGS WILL TURN OUT FOR THE BEST."

Martin, also from chapter 6, exuded a type of optimism that actually interfered with his coping process and significantly differed from the preferred form of can-do optimism expressed in hardy attitudes. His naive, complacent form of optimism obstructed his efforts to learn from his experience. Instead, it led to a pattern of denial that ended up costing him one sales job after another. Astonishingly, he responded to these reversals in fortune with a tolerant attitude that accommodated his denial. The laissez-faire attitude shown by Martin is one telltale sign of regressive coping.

In an effort to increase its customer base, one of the companies for which Martin worked put him and the entire sales crew through hardiness training. The company wanted its sales staff to develop resilient ways to cope with the stress of developing a larger customer base. Early in the group sessions, we asked course participants to jot down what they deemed the most stressful aspects of their jobs. They then shared this with the other group members.

Martin went first. He saw his work task as doable and could not think of any aspect of it that felt stressful to him. But strangely enough, as others spoke up, Martin agreed with their take on what caused them stress in their jobs. He said repeatedly, "Oh, I have that too." And then, he wrapped up his take on each stressful aspect with, "But, I can handle it because I keep a positive attitude." At the least, he was able to acknowledge that he experienced the stress his fellow coworkers experienced, despite his need to put a positive spin on all of it.

Martin observed his coworkers progressively working through their stress by using the transformational coping exercises. They took a broad perspective of their problems and made an effort to deepen their understanding of them. Their efforts were fruitful, as they found ways to positively resolve their problems and decrease the stressfulness of their circumstances.

Martin did not progress in the same way. By observing others, he began to recognize this. Soon, he admitted that if he had taken what was happening to him more seriously, he might have been able to keep jobs and get ahead, rather than to shift from one company to another without success or advancement. A great insight came to him when he realized that he had approached hardiness training in the same way. Chapter 8 talks about how transformational coping exercises helped Martin to move beyond his limitations.

HERMAN W.: "EVEN WHEN YOU HAVE THE CAREER YOU WANT, YOU MAY LOSE IT ALL AT ANY MOMENT."

After receiving his MBA degree, Herman started working as a human resources manager in a large, international company. Many years of hard work moved him up slowly through the ranks. After twenty-three years of service, he became vice president of the company's local branch and director of its human resources department. Above everything else, Herman valued stability and predictability in his professional and personal life. At this point, he had everything he wanted; he was stable and secure. Work peers and subordinates saw him as responsible, sincere, and straightforward.

Herman's interest in and involvement with other people and his work situations showed his attitude of commitment. But, his excessive need for professional and personal stability, predictability, and safety undermined his drive to seek and learn from new experiences. This weakened in him in the hardy attitudes of control and challenge.

Where did Herman's need for safety and predictability begin? He grew up in a middle-class family, wherein he and his siblings felt secure, despite the regular absence of his parents as they were often away at work, ensuring the family's financial security. He did well in school, and he is still in touch with former classmates. After casually dating two

girls in college, he met and married his wife. They have
been together ever since. Their two girls are now in late
adolescence. They have a rich family life and regularly do
things together, such as going to church, movies, and festi-
vals, and on vacations.

Generally, Herman built his life on stability, predictability, and security, as if change had no worthwhile role. His
worries and preoccupations were few in the safe and unchanging life he had built. Imagine how he felt when, one
fine day, the company's Executive Committee called him in
and announced that they had terminated the human resources function at that branch, and hence, he no longer
had a job!

Herman was devastated. He remembered all those job
offers he had turned down over the years. Why would anyone want to leave a stable company? He could not understand how his peers, whom he had known for so many
years, could do such a thing to him. He did not know what
to tell his wife and children, who had become accustomed
to a safe, predictable life. He began to reconsider all of his
choices and judgments over the years. Now, he felt bitter
and cynical about corporate America and people in general.

The meaning Herman applied to his life began to un-
ravel. After all, he had long since come to the conclusion
that stability and safety is the essence of a good life. Shortly
before he lost his job, his company offered employees
hardiness training. Chapter 8 talks about what Herman
learned by going through this training and the difference it
made in his life.

SUSAN M.: "I'M NOT PUTTING UP WITH THIS. IF THEY CAN'T TREAT ME WITH MORE RESPECT, I'M GETTING OUT OF HERE."

Each morning, Susan got ready for work. Besides her lunch,
cell phone, organizer, and other work paraphernalia, she

carried mental images of a model employee, coworker, supervisor, and employer. These snapshots stored well-defined ideas, themes, and story lines that strongly influenced how she related to work circumstances. Whenever she encountered stressful changes that challenged what she expected of a person or situation, she insisted on holding on to her well-defined models of the world.

Susan was a vice president in a small mortgage company that others in the industry regarded as maverick. It enjoyed several decades of success cornering its market share through this image. Like many of her coworkers, she enjoyed the boutique nature of the company and the business practices that stemmed from it. Her unconventional personality echoed the company's image, goals, and motivation, which positively contributed to her professional success.

Susan, caught up in the glory of the company's good-old days, was unprepared when global economic trends forced the company into a corporate merger that subordinated its management and functions. The company identity and procedures changed through a move to standardize and streamline products. This changed the small maverick company that shaped and discarded policies with each new deal, into a conventional and predictable place to work.

Susan felt lost and bitter about what she perceived as downward and sterile company changes. Management stopped inviting her to meetings. She knew less and less about company proceedings. In addition, her department had to do more with much less, which imposed greater workloads on those employees who survived the cuts. And, to add insult to injury, the new parent company no longer allowed vice presidents to come and go as they pleased. As in lower administrative echelons, she now had an eight-to-five job.

Susan viewed such changes as disrespectful to her, especially because she had all along been a loyal employee. She was bitter and resentful. Rather than think through the changes that stressed her, she let angry preoccupations consume her heart and mind. Susan saw the merger as lowering the company's principles and, self-righteously, she let them know this. She began to find any excuse to leave work early or to take the day off. She gave less of herself to her job and justified doing so by overemphasizing office scandals that, to her, confirmed the demise of the company's morals. This she was clear about. But, when it came to herself, Susan had less understanding. She knew what was wrong with the company, and how to change it, but never thought of changing herself.

1. *What might Susan need in order to change herself?*

As a youngster, Susan had raised herself. Her father had left the family when she was five years old. And, her mother favored alcohol over the care of her children. Susan became her brother's keeper, so to speak, and learned early on how to care for herself and others. The caretaking role eventually became second nature to her.

The combination of Susan's intellect, talent, and take-charge spirit gained the favor of management at her company, which helped her to rise up its ranks. Like the company, she was a maverick and flourished in work conditions that supported this expression. When the company changed, she did not take easily to being locked out of the game and made to feel like just one of the employees. There was no longer a match between Susan's values, goals, and motivations, and those of her employer.

Susan's insecurities lie dormant in the shadows of superiority and excellence. It never occurred to her that she was the one who needed to change. Her previous successes obscured the possibility of changing herself in the midst of these difficult, ongoing organizational changes.

2. Besides the obvious stress of company changes, what was Susan's problem?

Susan faced company changes at the same level of thinking that once helped her to survive, understand, and take charge in unsupportive circumstances. She coped with unreasonable childhood conditions by taking over and eventually leaving home at the age of seventeen; she never turned back. If she could, Susan would leave the company right now. But, she is three years away from retirement, and if she left today, she would lose a well-deserved retirement pension. In addition, Susan faced the fact that she no longer had the energy she had when she was seventeen. She felt trapped by the circumstance, blamed the company for her woes, and saw little possibility in this bleak situation. Clearly, she was stuck between a rock and a hard place. In this situation, changing herself was the only feasible option.

Susan did finally muster up the courage and found a way to make her job work for the next three years. She was still a valued employee, and she enjoyed fostering the talents of those she supervised. She realized that it was the training and development of others, and the friendships she formed in the process, rather than the perks, that kept her at this job for twenty-five years.

The transformational coping process helped Susan to recognize all of this. "I complained incessantly for months about the loss of my status, but when all is said and done, I'm a girl from Idaho who enjoys working with the ranks and making things happen." From that point on, Susan focused on work aspects that gave her pleasure and meaning. True to her leadership spirit, she used the knowledge and wisdom she gained to help those she supervised successfully navigate ongoing company changes.

What happened to Susan is an excellent example of how stressful changes can throw us off course if we are not resilient. But it also serves as a powerful case study of how transformational coping skills enable us to overcome disruptive change.

3. *What is the moral to Susan's story?*

If we all agreed on everything, there would be little incentive to question what we learned in the past and move beyond it. Such a scenario may be less stressful, but certainly, it does not foster growth and fulfillment. Today, disagreements between you and your employer in values, goals, and motivations are much more likely, as ever-changing shifts in corporate structure and operations widen the gulf between organizational and individual needs. The workplace today bears little resemblance to the workplace many once knew. Now, more than ever before, disruptive changes bring to the surface disagreements and conflicts that provoke you to come to terms with what is really going on and what you need to do about it.

WHERE DO YOU FIT IN?

Take a few minutes to answer the following questions as "True" or "False" in order to get a concrete sense of your way of dealing with stressful work changes, now and in the past. Remember, no one will see your answers but you, so be as honest as you can.

TRANSFORMATIONAL COPING

1. Do you immerse yourself in workplace changes to grasp their implications for you and your company?

2. Do you try to see how workplace changes can improve your functioning?

3. Do you try to see which directions workplace changes move you and your company?

4. Do you try to think through how you can plan to take advantage of workplace changes?

5. Do you try to carry out the plans to improve yourself in response to workplace changes?

6. If you try to carry out plans to improve yourself, do you open yourself up to feedback from your efforts to evaluate the effectiveness of your plan?

REGRESSIVE COPING

1. Do you see workplace changes as an unfortunate imposition and try to keep functioning the way you have been all along?

2. Do you try to bring back the good-old days?

3. Do you engage in distractions, such as watching a lot of television, so that you don't have to think about work problems?

4. Do you think that whatever is going to happen, will happen, and that you cannot really influence it?

5. When workplace changes happen, do you turn to others to find out what to do?

6. Do all of the ongoing changes make you wish you could just stop working?

To score your answers, give yourself one point for each time you answered "True" to a question. In order to see your approach to coping, total your scores for each set of six questions. Which set gave you the highest score, Transformational Coping or Regressive Coping? Keep these results in mind as you read further.

────── SUMMARY ──────

What the examples we have just presented show is that stressful circumstances can provoke regressive coping, especially if your hardy attitudes are already pretty low. This is the case with Allan H., Grace H., Martin O., and Susan M., who were not resilient under stress. Allan's life deteriorated when he resisted finding ways to restore purpose and meaning. Although Grace and Martin fared better than Allan did, their bitterness and self-pity engulfed them, sapping their courage and motivation to deal effectively with their stress. Grace and Susan blamed others for their problems. Martin, on the other hand, arranged to look the other way.

As shown by Herman's case, even if your hardy attitudes are moderate rather than low (remember, he was strong in commitment), a very stressful circumstance can lead to regressive coping unless you are careful to avoid this. Herman was beginning to blame others and the system, rather than working to solve the problem through transformational coping.

Clearly, when stressful circumstances confront you, you need to be ready and able to engage in transformational coping, as shown in the examples of Joey and Ruth earlier in the chapter. Otherwise, you risk meaninglessness, weakened resilience, and increased bitterness and self-pity. Chapter 8 shows you how to engage in the specifics of transformational coping. This form of coping is a useful technique to build yourself up by your effective reaction to stress, rather than by letting it knock you down.

PRACTICING TRANSFORMATIONAL COPING

Now that we have given some good examples of how transformational coping has been used to handle stressful circumstances, it is time to try this process yourself. There are three steps that help you to face stress. These steps utilize incisive analyses and constructive action to turn potential disasters into opportunities. In this chapter, we'll show you these steps and how to practice them. This is what it means to learn by doing. Then, once you supplement this by using the resulting feedback to deepen your hardy attitudes, you will have the courage and motivation to continue this resilient coping pattern throughout your life.

This process is a powerful advantage over the regressive coping strategies of denial and avoidance, or reacting catastrophically and striking out, described in earlier chapters. These regressive coping approaches are a direct, but primitive, expression of the fight-or-flight reaction that surfaces when we experience stressful circumstances. Striking out or avoiding may have been the best we humans could do when we were living in the wild. Now that we are civilized, and others expect us to be responsible, lawful, dependable, and resilient, any initial attraction to fighting or running away pales quickly as a coping strategy as this only makes things worse in the long run.

STEP ONE
LIST THE UNRESOLVED STRESSFUL CIRCUMSTANCES IN YOUR LIFE

Be as forthright and complete as you can, as this list is just for you; others will not see it, unless you want them to. Make sure that the items on the list are current, unsolved problems, rather than ones that no longer trouble you.

With regard to each stressful circumstance on your list, indicate whether it relates directly or indirectly to your work. Stressful circumstances that involve fellow employees, workplace tasks, company rules, changes in job definition, or job insecurity relate directly to work. Examples might include pressure on you to learn new procedures or to take on more work as the result of job redefinition or decreased workforce in your company. Or, perhaps you and your supervisor do not get along and have very different views of what you should be doing at work. Other kinds of stress, such as pervasive and preoccupying problems at home or in your private life, may indirectly interfere with your performance at work. For example, you may suspect that your spouse is having an affair, and this preoccupation makes it hard to involve yourself in your work. Or, perhaps your child has a behavior problem at school that requires so much time and attention, you are unable to fulfill your responsibilities at work.

Once you have made a list of all your stressful circumstances, reflect on and record the magnitude of each of them. Is the stress little more than an annoyance and therefore minor? An example might be the nuisance of having to make occasional paper recordings of particular work activities. Or, is the stress such a pervasive preoccupation that it can undermine your entire life? Here, an example might involve the ongoing pressure of having to terminate person after person in your department, as the company continues to downsize and reorganize. Use a scale from 1 (minor) to 7 (extremely major).

It is fine to estimate a stressful circumstance's magnitude subjectively. After all, this task of listing stressful circumstances is all about your experience of the world. But, if you need help with determining the magnitude of a stressful circumstance, let us make a suggestion. We call it the *ABCs of human needs*. These are needs we all share:

- A is for *accomplishment*. We all need to feel that we are getting things done and reaching worthwhile goals.

- B is for *belonging*. We all need to interact with others in such a way that our relationship with them influences our definition of who we are.

- C is for *comfort*. We all need to feel some degree of security so that we can relax and be calm and safe.

- D is for *dependability*. We all need a certain amount of predictability and regularity in our ongoing lives.

- E is for *esteem*. We all need to feel reasonably good about ourselves.

- Finally, F is for *finances*. We all need enough funds to lead a fulfilling life.

One way of determining the magnitude of a stressful circumstance is to ask yourself how many of these basic human needs it violates.

Finally, for each of the circumstances on your list, reflect on and record whether it is *acute* or *chronic*. It is acute if it represents a change from an ongoing steady state, such as having a computer file you were working on suddenly disappear or your boss firing you without warning. It is chronic if it involves a continuing mis-match between what you want and what you get. Perhaps you think of yourself as a creative person, but you're stuck in a routine job, or you want to be liked by coworkers, but feel continually rejected.

When you have listed all your stressful circumstances and de-scribed them in the ways we suggest, you will have before you a map of your present problems as they involve your work. You will know the stress you face, and this is the take-off point for doing something about it.

STEP TWO
THINK THROUGH EACH STRESSFUL CIRCUMSTANCE IN A WAY THAT BROADENS YOUR PERSPECTIVE AND DEEPENS YOUR UNDERSTANDING OF IT

This step is done by applying our Situational Reconstruction exer-cise to each stressful circumstance on your list. Which circum-stance do you start with? That's up to you. Some people start with a minor one so that they can concentrate on the exercise itself to learn how to do it well. Others start with a major one, because it preoccupies and undermines them so much that they need to re-solve it before anything else is done. Start with whichever stressful circumstance feels right, keeping in mind that, eventually, you are going to work on and resolve them all.

FINDING ALTERNATIVES (SPADING UP THE GROUND)

The exercise of Situational Reconstruction provides you with a set of questions to answer concerning your stressful circumstance. Answering these questions is a little like spading up the ground, to see what you find there and what the alternatives are. You will be enlisting your imagination in order to see the various ramifications and possibilities posed by the stressor and your interactions with it.

Question 1: What is your best description of the stressful circumstance you wish to solve?

Reflect on it and describe it as fully as you can. What are the problematic components of this circumstance? Who are the people involved? What are the likely implications or effects of this situation? What, in particular, is troublesome to you about all this? In particular, how does the stressful circumstance make you feel?

Question 2: Think of a way in which the stressful circumstance could be worse than it is.

Just let your imagination go and come up with a situation that would be worse. If your supervisor has criticized your performance, for example, it would be worse if you were fired for incompetence. The important thing about this step is that you identify what, for you, would be worse than the present problem.

Question 3: Think of a way in which the stressful circumstance could be better than it is.

Once again, let your imagination go and come up with a situation that is better than what is actually happening. For example, if your supervisor has criticized your performance, it would be better if she sent you for additional training to improve. Whatever the circumstance, you need to recognize what would make your present problem better.

Question 4: Make up a story about how the worse version of the stressful circumstance you identified in Question 2 would actually take place.

Here is where you really have to let your imagination go. Become a novelist with your own life. For this worse version of the stressful circumstance to take place, what would have to change?

Do you or others have to act differently? If so, then how? Does the situation, or the tasks involved, or the roles you and others play have to be different? If so, then how? Observe yourself doing this task. It will help you understand, concretely, your perception of how bad things happen.

Once you have finished the story, estimate (on a scale from 0 to 100 percent) how likely it is to come true. It's somewhat reassuring if the likelihood is small, as the probability is low that the situation will get out of control. But don't be too reassured. After all, the circumstance is already stressful and problematic, so you can't afford to be lulled into complacency just because it may not get worse. And, if the likelihood of the circumstance getting worse is high, then it certainly should have a high priority in your efforts to improve your life.

Question 5: Make up a story about how the better version of the stressful circumstance would actually take place.

Once again, really let your imagination go. What would have to change in order for this better version to happen? Do you or others have to act differently? If so, then how? Does the situation, or the tasks involved, or the roles you and others play have to be different, and if so, then how? Observe yourself doing this task. It will help you understand, concretely, your perception of how good things happen.

Once you have finished the story, estimate (on a scale from 0 to 100 percent) how likely it is to occur. If the likelihood is small, then that is even more reason to throw yourself into solving the problem, for it will certainly not happen on its own. If it is highly likely that you can solve it, though, that does not mean that you can afford to ignore it. Rather, you should encourage yourself to think that your efforts are worth it, as they are likely to bring success.

Question 6: What specifically can you personally do to bring about the better version of your problem and prevent the worse version from happening?

You may have answered this already in completing the previous two questions, but here is another opportunity to imagine how you might be proactive in coping with the stressful circumstance. Even though you may have inserted yourself into the scenarios whereby the problem becomes better or worse, it is time now to reflect further on what you can do to promote success. Do you need to take certain actions, convince others of the value of something, seek additional information and assistance, or make sure you stand your ground? Answering this question is a chance to reflect on your sense of possibilities once again.

Searching for Perspective and Understanding

In answering the first six questions of Situational Reconstruction, you have spaded up the ground of the stressful circumstance to see how it helps your thoughts on the problem you now confront. The next three questions address this reflective process.

Question 7: Based on what you learned by answering the previous questions, can you find a way to place this stressful circumstance into perspective?

Coping with the stressful circumstance may arouse painful emotions. Here, you may actually increase painful emotions temporarily. You may feel anxious, angry, depressed, suspicious, or all of these. On the other hand, if you have moved toward a solution in your efforts to answer the first six questions of Situational Reconstruction, you may feel a bit better. In either case, it is especially important for you to find a way to put the circumstance in perspective; that is, find a way to make sense out of it.

There is a lot at stake here. When you put a problem in perspective, it becomes tolerable, even though it is not yet resolved. And, because it is tolerable, you can mull it over, figure out a course of action, and then take the necessary measures. Without this perspective, the problem may repel you when you think about it, making it harder to think through possible solutions.

Five Frequently Used Perspectives

Perhaps you can find a perspective on your own, building on the work you have done thus far. In case you have trouble, however, there are five forms of perspective that are frequently used to help find feasible solutions to problems. Recognize that this is not a definitive list—you may well find an unmentioned perspective of your own. Or, you may feel that more than one form of perspective fits your situation. That's okay too. You don't need to restrict yourself to only one, as long as your conclusion makes sense to you.

1. COMMONPLACE PERSPECTIVE. Perhaps you have been thinking that you are the only one to have collided with the stressful circumstance at hand. Feeling alone while being undermined by a problem makes it harder to tolerate. It is especially easy, then, to sink into self-pity and bitterness. "Why me?" In contrast, you adopt the commonplace perspective when you recognize that others have experienced this type of stressful circumstance, now or in the past. Do you see how this commonplace perspective can make the stressful circumstance tolerable so that you can mull it over and take the necessary actions?

2. MANAGEABILITY PERSPECTIVE. By now, you have considered how the stressful circumstance could become better or worse. In other words, its actual status is somewhere in between these two extremes. This kind of thinking may encourage you to adopt the manageability perspective. In this, you feel heartened by realizing that the stressful circumstance is neither as bad nor as good as things can get in your life. When in childhood you went crying to your mother because an untrustworthy friend cast you off, did she tell you, "I know it hurts you, but you still have lots of trustworthy friends," to console you? That's the manageability perspective. In this perspective, you take the standpoint that the stressful circumstance always could be worse. This perspective makes the situation tolerable so you can approach it long enough to solve it.

3. IMPROVABILITY PERSPECTIVE. For this perspective, the stressful circumstance becomes more tolerable because you find a standpoint from which it can improve. You imagine ways to improve the circumstance rather than to just have passive optimism that does little to change it. This helps you to feel better as you struggle to resolve the situation.

4. TIME PERSPECTIVE. Another way to make the circumstance tolerable is to find a standpoint, based on the work you have done thus far, that helps you to see how the worst of it will be over in some reasonably definable time. Even if things are awful right now, that pain becomes more manageable and less disruptive if you can anticipate a time when all will be better. Perhaps the stressor involves some required, but overwhelming performance on your part that comes along with a deadline. If you can think of how things will calm down once the deadline has passed, it may help you to tolerate the pain and give the necessary effort to be successful.

5. UNPREDICTABILITY PERSPECTIVE. Although it seems to go against transformational coping ideas, this perspective is useful. Imagine that, despite your efforts to think through how to solve the problem, you recognize that you cannot resolve some of its aspects. You can do what you can to solve the problem, but the precise outcome is still somewhat unpredictable. For instance, consider when doctors give patients all the necessary treatments for a serious illness. Then, they have to tell patients' families that only time will tell whether their loved ones will live or die. The unpredictability perspective helps you to tolerate the stressful circumstance, if you know that you have done what you can to solve it. What happens from that point on is out of your hands.

Question 8: Based on what you have learned, do you now have a deeper understanding of how you can improve the stressful circumstance?

By answering the first six questions of Situational Reconstruction, you should have deepened your understanding of the stressful circumstance. Often, this process leads you to a clearer picture of what you have to do to solve the problem. Perhaps you will come out of this exercise with more subtle understandings of your situation. You may acquire a detailed sense of what the circumstance, or the basis for its stress, really is. You may even emerge from the exercise with a completely different take on what is making the situation problematic and stressful. The potential for a deeper understanding is the primary reason why it is worth the effort to answer the questions included in Situational Reconstruction.

Understanding Your Stressors

As with a broadened perspective, you may reach a deeper understanding on your own by going through this exercise. After all, there are many ways to understand how to handle stressful circumstances. Often, a circumstance becomes stressful in part because of our own particular ways of experiencing things. In other words, others may differ from you in their reaction to a stressful circumstance that you are all experiencing. If you need some guidance on how to deepen your understanding of your stressor, let us provide some frequently used ways to do so. These underlying meanings come up repeatedly among the people we have trained in hardiness. They are, however, by no means the only ways for understanding problems. You may find one or more of them make sense to you in your ongoing stressful situation.

■ **PERSONAL LIMITATION.** Perhaps someone else's actions caused your stressful circumstance. Or, unsympathetic organizational rules and policies led to your stress. But, as you immersed yourself in spading the ground through Situational Reconstruction, you found that you were the cause of the stress. However painful this process might be, you may be on the way to solving the problem constructively by recognizing your contribution to it.

If, from thinking things through, there emerges a sense that your own personal limitation is involved, face it honestly. Remember, the most important thing you are trying to accomplish is turning the stressor from a potential disaster into an opportunity. To do this, you must gain an accurate understanding, even if it is painful. Once you actually solve the problem by working constructively with your personal limitations, the pain of initially recognizing your limitations fades away.

■ MISUNDERSTANDINGS. You may come to the realization that misunderstood words or actions played a big role in bringing about the stressful circumstance. Maybe others involved did not grasp your meaning accurately. Or, maybe you misunderstood their words or actions. Even worse, it could be a combination of misunderstandings on all sides, yours and theirs. Often, such confusion builds, causes feelings of pain or anger, and results in disorganization and failure.

The upside of this is that, if it seems like a misunderstanding played an important role in the problem, then by recognizing this, you can make a huge difference in setting the situation right. If you misunderstood the words or actions of others, however hurtful or humiliating it may seem, you should face up to it courageously, so you both can move to solve it. If others misunderstood your words or actions, things will only worsen if you denigrate, shun, or strike out at them. Here, it's best to accept others' misunderstandings, so you can think through constructive ways to get beyond them.

■ CLASH OF WILLS. Sometimes, you may come to recognize that the stressfulness of the circumstance stems more from an out-and-out disagreement than from a misunderstanding. Your own and others' goals, values, or preferences lead to different approaches to understanding and solving stressful circumstances.

Here, a clash of wills produces the stressful circumstance. If this is true, once again, it is best to recognize and admit it, for this is the only way you can figure out effective ways to reduce the stressfulness of the situation. Without first recognizing the problem's true nature, down the road you have little chance of successfully resolving it.

■ VICTIMIZATION. It may seem to you that you have little to no responsibility for the stressful circumstance. Instead, you conclude that others victimized you by their desire to scapegoat or undermine you. Through no fault of your own, others ostracized, denigrated, discriminated against, or harassed you.

There are two important things to consider about this form of understanding. First, though it's dreadful to be victimized by others, you can still move beyond it and grow from the experience. It is clearly better to act constructively in this situation than to sink into powerlessness and self-pity. Second, it is best to avoid rushing prematurely to the conclusion that others have victimized you. Reaching this conclusion too easily may be little more than a way to avoid taking any responsibility for what has happened. As such, it will not help you to resolve the problem. It is best to go carefully through the first six questions of Situational Reconstruction, answering them in depth and detail. Then, if you still understand the problem as stemming from victimization, your conclusion may be legitimate.

■ EXTERNAL FORCES. Sometimes, as you spade up the ground through Situational Reconstruction, you may recognize that despite your own best efforts and the best efforts of others, there's little that can be done to reduce the stressfulness of the situation. Forces outside of your control may play a strong role in bringing about the situation. Technological advance, equal-opportunity pressures, and outsourced company functions are examples of stressful forces outside of your control. Rather than blaming yourself or blaming others, it's best to figure out if such forces influence the stressfulness of a problem. What can be done to decrease the stressfulness of a problem that is caused by external forces differs significantly from what can be done when you or others around you cause the problem.

Question 9: Is there a resolution in sight?

At this point, you have gone through all the questions of Situational Reconstruction that help you put the stressful circumstance in a broader perspective and deepen your understanding of it. Now, it is time for you to reflect on whether you have some sense of what you can do to improve the circumstance and to solve the problem inherent in it. You may feel better now that you can imagine a resolution. But, the change is only in your mind at this point, so you may still be feeling pain. After all, imagining a resolution is good, but it still has not yet come to fruition. This is even more reason for learning to bring about change in the problematic circumstance out there, where it exists, which is Step Three. But before we get there, let's look again at some actual case studies where people used Situational Reconstruction to help with their resilient coping.

SITUATIONAL RECONSTRUCTION CASE STUDIES

Do you now see alternative solutions to solving your problem? Do you think you can turn a stressful circumstance from adversely affecting you to an opportunity to learn and grow? The case studies that follow pick up the stories of Grace, Martin, and Herman and show you how Situational Reconstruction worked to their advantage.

GRACE H.

The transformational coping exercises described here did Grace a world of good. By focusing on her job status and relationship with her boss, Grace considered how it could be worse, and how it could be better. In doing this, she noted that at least the company hung on to her as an employee. She believed they valued her reliability and trustworthiness. "That's why they kept me on board," she thought. She also recognized that by increasingly alienating herself from coworkers, she undermined her motivation to work hard. In this regard, she estimated that she had a 50 percent chance of losing her job.

Grace chose a job promotion as the stressful circumstance's best-case scenario. She struggled diligently to temper her anger, bitterness, and self-pity, so she could approach and figure out how to bring about this desired goal. She had difficulty imagining her boss on his own considering her worthy enough to promote. She thus rated the likelihood of this best-case scenario at only 15 percent.

Through this Situational Reconstruction process, she admitted that she had to let go of her negative feelings about him, if she wanted to change her boss's view of her. And, rather than lick her wounds, and wait for others to tell her what to do, she would take initiative to help her boss and the company to master stressful work changes. She recognized that only by changing her negative attitudes and self-defeating behaviors could she make the job promotion happen. She used her new perspectives and understandings to develop a plan of action.

Which perspectives did she garner by reflecting upon what happened? First, Grace flirted with a victimization standpoint. Finally, she was able to see how she presented herself as a person who takes orders rather than as a person who makes things happen. If she failed to develop herself in this area, she would learn little about how to turn stressful problems to her advantage. Through this, she realized that her problem was commonplace, the difficulty many employees experience. More importantly, the problem involved mutual misunderstandings. The way Grace's boss treated her reminded her of the way she had been treated by her father. This led her to become defensive and detached and led her boss to perceive her as a follower, not a leader.

These insightful perspectives made the problem tolerable, allowing Grace to understand it more fully. With this deeper understanding, Grace realized a personal limitation she possessed, a limitation that need not be permanent, since she had gained insight into an alternative. Now, she was ready to make an Action Plan (Step Three) and carry it out.

MARTIN O.

In working on Situational Reconstruction, Martin had a hard time imagining anything worse than what was actually happening to him. After all, he had been unsuccessful and was fired repeatedly. But, he finally concluded that it would be even worse if his poor work record led other prospective employers to turn him down. He also began to admit that he contributed to this failure by not taking his situation seriously enough to do something about it. Overall, he anxiously attributed a 70 percent likelihood to this worst-case scenario.

As to how things could be better, Martin imagined himself as a successful salesperson, valued by his company, and sought after by prospective employers. Through broadening his perspective of the problem, he overcame his dismay and recognized how his passivity contributed to his circumstance. Through his intelligent and socially adept ways, he vowed to improve himself. He also gave a 70 percent rating to the likelihood of his bringing about this best-case scenario. By keeping his nose to the grindstone, he believed he could make this happen.

Through this Situational Reconstruction process, he recognized that it was he, not his supervisors, who would have to change. In particular, he would have to scrutinize his performance moment to moment, with the task in mind of how to be successful in garnering the sale. Martin recognized that his stressful circumstance stemmed from his naive optimism, a personal limitation. He was ready now to develop action-based strategies to make the best of his sales calls. He would incorporate the many points taught to him in former companies' sales training workshops that he once took less seriously.

HERMAN W.

The members of Herman's human resources department were going through hardiness training partly to help them understand its role in resiliency. Fortunately, the training was already going on when his company informed him that he no longer had a job. To Herman, a successful employee high up in the company's ranks, this event was cataclysmic. Recall that the company's efforts to cut costs had led it to outsource its human resource functions.

Herman told us tearfully, during a hardiness training session, that the company let him go. He stated, "The very same people who had been my friends and colleagues for twenty years told me today that I no longer have a job here. How could I have been so stupid as to think they were my friends?" Herman wondered if, all along, they planned to terminate him, and if he had performed much worse than he had realized. As he sank into bitterness and self-pity, we rallied around and supported him.

Nonetheless, Herman did not have the composure to struggle with Situational Reconstruction until the next training session. At that time, he had to consider a way in which his stressful circumstance could become worse. For him, a financial disaster would have done it, especially since his two daughters were college age. But, he saw that the reasonable severance package the company gave him prevented his financial situation from worsening. The only thing that would have kept him from getting such an ample severance package was if his former peers had not valued his contributions throughout the years. This made him wonder whether his former colleagues were really the enemies he initially thought them to be. He concluded that the likelihood of the worse scenario was only 10 percent.

Herman had a difficult time coming up with a better version of the stressful circumstance. He did suggest that by decreasing department budgets the company might have been able to keep human resource functions in-house. He did actually suggest this to his colleagues when they told him they would have to eliminate his job because of budget concerns. Rather than address his solution to the problem, his colleagues told Herman that they were just carrying out the Board of Directors' request, without much power to change it. Herman had considered their response to be a rationalization, although he did not voice this to them. He concluded that the only way this better version of the stressor could occur was if his colleagues, the Executive Committee, had the courage of their conviction to stand up to the Board of Directors. He thought the chances of this happening were only 10 percent.

Herman finally concluded that his problem involved a commonplace perspective. He, like many others in his department, lost their jobs through the decision to outsource human resource functions. As a way to understand what happened to him, he settled on external forces. Because of external pressures brought by market changes and investor requirements, the company had difficulty justifying the cost of keeping human resource functions within the company.

These conclusions led Herman to the only possible best-case scenario, which was to accept his job loss, and use the experience instead to jump-start a new career. Perhaps he could use his twenty-three years of human resources experience in a major company to either find a better job in another company, or go out on his own as a consultant. The latter might be the way to go, if other companies were likely to cut down on their in-house human resource functions at a time of dwindling revenues. He liked this best-case scenario and thought this had an 80 percent chance of happening. Clearly, only he could bring about this final scenario. He began to elaborate on it in his mind enthusiastically. Soon, it was time for an Action Plan.

STEP THREE
MAKE AN ACTION PLAN, CARRY IT OUT, AND PAY ATTENTION TO THE FEEDBACK YOU GET FROM YOUR COPING EFFORTS

Now that you have broadened your perspective and deepened your understanding of the stressful circumstance you are working on, you are ready to put together an Action Plan that follows from your thought process and could have a decisive effect on turning the problem to your advantage. It is not enough to let the relief you gained by thinking through the problem satisfy you. You need to turn your insights into strategic actions that transform the stressful circumstance out there, where it exists. In order to do this, you should now go through our Action Plan exercise. Be sure to answer each of the questions below.

Question 1: What is the goal of your action plan?

Although it may sound obvious, let us reinforce for you that the goal of your plan needs to follow from the deepened understanding you have achieved through Situational Reconstruction. It isn't relevant for the goal to be what others want you to do. Rather, it must reflect what you have learned by spading up the ground. Nor will it be effective to rush into something without being fully clear in your mind as to what you want to happen. "Ready, fire, aim" never helps. Your ultimate goal must guide your actions along the way.

Also, though some goals are more complex or abstract than others, it is important to be completely clear and detailed before doing anything. Let's say that your stressful circumstance is that you were passed over for a promotion, which the decision makers in the company gave to someone else. It isn't helpful to adopt the goal that everything will be better. A more clear, concrete, and helpful goal would be to make sure that the decision makers offer you a promotion the next time they look for someone. This goal already suggests actions you can take that can be instrumental. Your goal should be something that, if achieved, would end, or at the least decrease, the stressfulness of the circumstance and help you to grow in the process.

Question 2: What are the instrumental acts that will lead you to the goal?

It's difficult through just one effort to succeed in your goals. Therefore, it is necessary to think through the various actions that you need to take, each leading you closer to the ultimate goal. Write down these instrumental acts as concretely as you can, specifying what you need to do, how your actions bring you closer to the goal, and ways in which they involve other persons and circumstances. Usually, you need to sequence these instrumental acts for the action plan to be sound.

Following through on the example given above, let's say that your goal is to make sure that company decision makers promote you the next time there is a higher-level job opening. Your instrumental acts might include approaching each decision maker with your strong interest and work-task examples that show you working hard and making innovative decisions to improve company sales. You may decide to approach decision makers separately to increase the likelihood that they each notice you and your work contributions, efforts, and expertise.

As to sequencing these instrumental acts, you may decide to rank the decision makers in your mind as to how close you are to them already. Then, you may decide to start with the ones who know and value you already, and work your way to those who know you less, or not at all. You may choose this strategy partly because it minimizes the group's possible recognition of and opposition to your strategy, and partly because success at the beginning of your efforts will hearten you when approaching interactions that are more problematic.

Question 3: What is your timeline for each instrumental act?

Thus far, you specified your ultimate problem-solving goal, the instrumental acts necessary to reaching it, and the sequence in which they lead you to achieving your goal. Now, you should try to specify how long each of the instrumental steps is likely to take. This is important for two reasons.

First, it's unwise to lull yourself into thinking that now you know what needs to be done and you can do it at the drop of a hat. You may end up putting the Action Plan on the back burner, because you feel you can do it easily, whenever you want. Only, you may never quite get around to it.

Second, it's rare for people to be able to quickly carry out actions that effectively reduce a problem's stressfulness. A realistic estimate of the time each of the instrumental acts will take to accomplish will help you continue to carry through on your Action Plan and prevent you from throwing up your hands in frustration when the goal doesn't come immediately.

It may be next to impossible to be very precise about your timeline. But, the effort to make one and stick to it will be helpful to you.

ACTION PLAN REVISION

Action plans need to be organic, flexible strategies. If the added information you get from one or more of the instrumental acts of your plan suggests that your strategy or timeline needs to be altered, do not hesitate to do so. The reactions you get to a particular act may tell you that it will take longer to accomplish than you thought. Or, that it may have to be modified to incorporate something you had not anticipated. It is even possible that, under some circumstances, your overall goal will need fine-tuning or slight modification. But, if you consider making changes to your Action Plan, make sure that you are being honest and straightforward with yourself, and not just placating yourself by ignoring and denying the difficulties of what you are trying to accomplish.

THREE SOURCES OF FEEDBACK THAT DEEPEN YOUR RESILIENCE

As you take the instrumental steps of your Action Plan, you need to be very aware of the feedback you get from your efforts. It is this feedback that will deepen your hardy attitudes, so that when you are done with this book, and no longer have us looking over your shoulder, you will have your own courage and motivation to cope with stressful circumstances you encounter in the future.

There are three sources of feedback to the actions guided by your plan:

1. **PERSONAL REFLECTIONS.** The first source of feedback is the observations you make of yourself in action. You might ask, "Wow, is that really me? I didn't know I could really do that," or, "Why didn't I think of doing this before?" Or, you might observe, "This didn't work completely, but it's a lot better than what was happening before." You will see yourself doing what is needed.

2. **OTHER PEOPLE.** Another source of feedback is the observations of your actions made by others. They may tell you, "I didn't think you had the guts to say that to our boss. I know I don't. I'm proud of you," or, "You're like a different person—so strong and decisive. What has happened?" Sometimes, a person around you may seem jealous of your decisive actions. But, if you stop to think about it, you will realize that a person's jealousy probably reveals his envy of you. The feedback is still that you are great.

3. **RESULTS.** The third source of feedback is the actual effects of your actions on the intended target. Maybe you dispelled misunderstandings by mutually exploring each other's viewpoints. If this works out well, you reap wonderful benefits from your actions.

The value of attending carefully to these sources of feedback is that they can deepen your hardy attitudes. If the feedback is positive, you will feel more involved in and less alienated from the stressful circumstance. You will also feel more in control and learn from the challenge your efforts represent, rather than being threatened by it all. You will emerge from the situation not only having improved it, but also feeling more commitment, control, and challenge in it. These hardy attitudes will begin to generalize beyond the particular situation to others in your present or future. Before you know it, you will have all the courage and motivation you need to be resilient and make your life fulfilling.

EXAMPLES OF THE BENEFITS OF FEEDBACK

We hope you are curious as to what happened to Grace H., Martin O., and Herman W., when they got to the point of formulating their Action Plans and actually taking the steps involved. Here's a summary of their processes:

Grace H. Her efforts with Situational Reconstruction led her to an Action Plan to be proactive in her job. As she laid out the steps she would take to make a more significant contribution to the company—beyond just working hard—she realized how passive she had let herself become.

Soon, in carrying out her Action Plan, Grace was making notes on how she could improve company operations and was initiating regular meetings with her boss to discuss these suggestions with him. After a while, he actually began coming to her with questions and problems, asking for her suggestions on possible solutions. Before long, they were a team, rather than just two people working in the same office. Then, Grace got her promotion—she became office manager.

In this transformational coping process, Grace got lots of positive feedback. She saw herself rising above her misgivings and being proactive. Others at the company showed renewed interest in her, complimenting her on her suggestions and efforts. And, of course, her boss began turning to her for help in solving problems. As a result of all this feedback, she began to say, "I can get ahead at work if I take the initiative to make contributions and don't spend my time bogged down worrying about whether this is a man's world."

So, her hardy attitudes were also increasing. She felt much more committed to, and less withdrawn from, the work world around her. Further, she thought that by taking the initiative, rather than sinking into passivity and powerlessness, she could have an influence on the things going on around her. Whether or not this was the best job in the world for her mattered less, because she used her experiences as a guide to continually improve and felt more fulfilled in the process.

And, before long, she was engaging in transformational coping with regard to the other stressful circumstances in her life. Soon, this process was a new way of life for her, and she felt so good about interacting with the world around her, even if the problems she had to tackle were difficult.

Martin O. After formulating his Action Plan, he began using it in his sales efforts. For six months, he chose to double his sales calls until they reached the level recommended by his company. He would plan each encounter with a prospective customer, making clear to himself the person's needs, likes, and dislikes, and the best ways to present the company's products that matched the customer's requirements.

Further, he reached out to the prospective customer, both in the initial meeting and in the follow-up interactions he initiated. It was not surprising to us that, when he began using this new strategy, his success rate improved to the point where his supervisor was very pleased with him. After all, Martin was both intelligent and gregarious. And, now that he was prepared and able to evaluate his performance and change it according to his sales goals, he had the final ingredient for success.

The feedback he got from observing himself was awesome. For the first time in his life, he saw himself in his interactions with the world clearly. It was so interesting for him and gave him so much information to work with. Further, his supervisor finally had reason to give Martin positive feedback. And of course, Martin did not fail to recognize that his sales record kept improving.

Because of his old pattern of taking it easy, we had to encourage Martin to keep using the resilient coping techniques he had learned on the other stressful circumstances he was experiencing. Through his more effective efforts, he began turning his entire life around and felt proud.

Before long, Martin was showing strong hardy attitudes of commitment, control, and challenge, rather than his lackluster, undiscerning detachment of the past. He would often say, "You have to see your stressful problems clearly in order to do anything about them. My long-standing naive optimism just got in the way of my development." His dramatic turnaround was very exciting to us all.

Herman W. The goal of his Action Plan was to engage in work that enhanced his career and preserved financial security, despite having lost his job. Herman acted in two ways that were instrumental to achieving his goals. Looking for another job was one key action toward Herman's goal. He enlisted a recruiter to help him, networked with long-term business associates, and systematically attended human resources conventions to look for leads. He learned a lot in this process, which encouraged him to begin his own consulting company.

Herman also took a courageous step by visiting the same colleagues who had let him go, telling them of his plans and asking for their business support. After all, they were in need of outside human resources services, and Herman knew their business inside and out. In trying to convince them, he relied on his solid reputation and strong work relationships with them. If they went with him, that would provide him with the needed start-up funding to finance his new business

Imagine how Herman felt when the Executive Committee voted unanimously to be his first customer. He confirmed through his effort that, in fact, the company planned to outsource human resource functions for the reasons they gave to Herman. Also, the executive committee members had always respected his capabilities and knowledge and could now feel less guilty about terminating his employment. After this decisive success, Herman actually gave up looking for work in another company.

With growing enthusiasm and sense of personal worth, Herman began organizing the implementation of human resource functions for his old company and searching for new customers. He had, soon, a number of additional clients, a handsome office near his home, and the support of his wife and several former colleagues who now worked alongside him. Others unanimously agreed that Herman turned his stressful problem to his advantage.

He got this feedback by observing his own actions, receiving others' feedback as to his efforts, and realizing the many positive effects brought about through his coping efforts. He rose above defeat to fulfilling his values and capabilities in new ways he never imagined. His hardy attitudes rose to a level that he had never achieved before.

When we last heard from him, he was making more money than when he was in the company, and had gone from worrying about how to send his children to college to wondering why he had not thought of going out on his own before. He also felt great about being his own boss and believed that being fired was a wonderful wake-up call for his career and life. In terms of attitudes, he had gone from anger, self-pity, and pessimism, to the commitment, control, and challenge we have been emphasizing.

CONTINUE THE TRANSFORMATIONAL COPING PROCESS

By now, you have seen how the people we used as examples turned their stressful circumstances from potential disasters into opportunities through the transformational coping process. Hopefully, you too have had success in your own initial attempt with this procedure. It is important to keep this process going.

When you finish working on the first stressful circumstance, choose another one from your list, using the same coping process. Keep clearing away stressful circumstances through transformational coping until you can truthfully say that, on an ongoing basis, you are resiliently managing stressful life changes. The amount of success you have in your coping efforts may vary from one stressful circumstance to another. But, you can be sure that, in general, your life will be much less stressful, and more successful. Workplace problems will seem like no big deal as you continue to turn them to your advantage. Life is like riding a bicycle: If you keep pedaling, you move forward.

SUMMARY

It is not enough for someone to tell us what we should believe and do. Indeed, this may make us even more cynical, or at least keep us wondering what's wrong with us for not being able to make a difference. It would never have worked for us to tell Grace, Martin, and Herman what they needed to do in order to become more resilient. To change, all of us have to engage in behaviors that bring about solutions to problems. This simultaneously convinces us that the world around us can be more like what we had hoped.

By now, we have come a good distance in building resilience through hardiness. In chapters 5 and 6, we covered how to increase your hardy attitudes of commitment, control, and challenge. And, in chapters 7 and 8, we covered how to engage in transformational coping to better turn stressful circumstances from potential disasters into opportunities. If you maintain these processes, you will see what an important difference you can make in your life.

Another important aspect of resilience at work is to build social support by giving and receiving assistance and encouragement with the significant people in your life. In chapters 9 and 10, we'll show you how.

CHAPTER 9

SOCIAL SUPPORT: GIVING AND RECEIVING ASSISTANCE AND ENCOURAGEMENT

"We make a living by what we get.
We make a life by what we give."

—W. A. NANCE[1]

So far we've mostly discussed how you can build resilience and coping skills from within. Now let's turn to the importance of giving and receiving social support—another key to resiliency. Think of the fellow employees with whom you interact on a daily basis. For that matter, think also of your family members, friends, and other people who matter to you. How would you like your relationship to be with these people?

Would you like to compete with them all the time? Suppose it's a continual question of who gets ahead or falls behind, and that determines your worth. You can never let your guard down and relax, to say nothing of working cooperatively with them.

They will trump you and never let you forget that you lost, if you let them. Would you like the people you work with and those who are so close to you to have this relentlessly competitive quality?

If the pattern of competition were subtle and covert, would that make it any better? Although the person is significant in your life, you would never be able to trust him or her, because there might be a concealed plot to upstage you when you least expect it. And, you would feel as if you had to try to undermine the person before the person undermined you. If anything, subtle competitiveness undermines you more than competitiveness in its more obvious form.

What follows are examples of two people who came to us for hardiness training, unaware of the debilitating lack of social support present in their work situations.

DAVID G.

This young man could not understand why he became so tense every time he came to work. Upon entering the building of his high-tech employer, he would become anxious, his heart would race, his stomach would rumble, and he would begin thinking how in the world he could get his work done well. His work team was composed of equally young employees, all of whom had extensive computer training and looked forward to distinguished, lucrative careers.

As he described the situation, it became clear that the team members, including him, did not really help each other accomplish the group's goals. Covertly, each believed that if anyone was promoted, it should be him or her. This led each of them to try to undermine the others, sometimes subtly and sometimes not so subtly, even to the point of

---

erasing each other's work computer files. This was destructive for both the employees and the company.

What's the worst that could happen if one of these team members helped, rather than tried to undermine the others? Someone else might get the promotion (though this is hardly a foregone conclusion). But, even if this happened, who would that promoted person turn to as a trusted associate? None other than the helpful team member, because of the assistance provided prior to the promotion.

Competition among employees that decreases social support undermines everyone's performance and health.[2] Interestingly, overprotection often produces similar results. Whenever there is a difficult situation, an overprotector will take it out of his coworkers' hands and deal with it himself, instead of helping the others learn how to take the needed action. Although they may feel better in the short term because the problem has been solved, they will never come to be effective themselves. Under such circumstances, it will be hard for them to build confidence in their ability to perform well at work. Instead, they will feel increasingly dependent on the overprotector, all the while building up resentment toward him because they can't get along without him. And, if you were the overprotective one, you would be encouraging those you protected to resent you because they couldn't get along without you.

JANE W.

Jane considered herself just one of many accountants in a large manufacturing firm, but she could not understand why she felt bored by her job. As she described her work situation more completely, it became clear that her boss was an overprotective supervisor. He made all of the decisions, took on any complicated work himself, and left the routine stuff for the others, including Jane, to do. Jane described him as an admirable, hard-working, nurturing boss on the one hand.

On the other hand, however, there was an accumulation of resentment underneath this admiration. Jane felt not only powerless, but also trivialized. Although she was always getting praise and merit increases from the company, no one even knew her, and the years were going by without her position improving. Soon, she recognized that her overprotective boss was the reason for her dissatisfaction with her life.

BUILDING TWO-WAY SOCIAL SUPPORT

In contrast to the examples of David and Jane, you and those with whom you work closely need to deepen and treasure your ongoing relationships. You need to be able to count on each other in addressing work situations, without having to wonder what you can expect. The way to do this is by entering into a pattern of interaction with them where assistance and encouragement are exchanged and there is little competition or overprotection.

This may seem hard. After all, each relationship has a history that may not easily lend itself to exchanging assistance and encouragement. But, what needs to be done is actually easier than it might seem. All you need to do is take the first step in giving the other person assistance and encouragement. Then, it will be very difficult for the person not to follow suit. And, before you know it, the relationship will be more secure, satisfying, and lead to more effective job performance for you both. That is the way of social support and it helps build a foundation of resiliency.

Specifically, what's involved in the social support concept of encouraging and assisting someone who is struggling with stressful changes? One aspect of encouragement is empathy, which is putting yourself in the other person's shoes, feeling and thinking about the situation as she does. Empathy leads to another aspect of encouragement, namely, sympathy. Once you know how the other person is feeling and thinking, you know the pain she is experiencing. Expressing sympathy for this pain can actually help the other person tolerate it. Yet another aspect of encouragement is showing appreciation for the person, by communicating your faith in her ability to deal with the problems.

One aspect of assistance involves taking up the slack, by temporarily helping with the other person's responsibilities when pressures and unexpected changes overwhelm her. The second aspect of assistance is giving the person some breathing room to deal with the mounting pressures. The final aspect of assistance involves offering your particular resources (such as relevant knowledge, expertise, or contacts) if that is what is needed to facilitate the person's dealing effectively with the stressful changes. Taking the first steps in offering assistance and encouragement is what chapter 10 is about.

CASE STUDIES ON SOCIAL SUPPORT

Let's turn first to some examples of specific ways in which relationships are commonly undermined by competition or overprotection, making it more difficult to deal effectively with stressful changes. What follows is based on many years of coaching people on how to improve interactions with coworkers, family, and friends.

BILL F.: "I DON'T HAVE STRESS, I ONLY GIVE IT!"

Bill's company sent him for hardiness training. A department head in a large financial firm, Bill had excellent work-task capabilities, the basis on which he might have expected further promotions. His managerial skills, however, left much to be desired. His subordinates disliked working under his supervision, felt underappreciated and vulnerable, complained behind the scenes, and often transferred or left the company. His peers saw him as aloof and full of himself. His supervisors were understandably worried—hence, they called us in.

As we talked with him about his work interactions, Bill stated the problem clearly by saying, "When someone doesn't perform well, I lace into them. But, when someone does a good job, I don't feel the need to reward them, because they are just doing what they're being paid for." Later in our discussions, when we were trying to sympathize with him about the enormous stress he was under, he blurted out proudly, "I don't have stress, I give it!"

It was clear that, in Bill's view, punishing subordinates and imposing unreachable goals on them is the best way to get them to perform well. And, he didn't want to praise or otherwise reward them when they did a good job, for fear that they would then become complacent.

More than Bill realized, he took a competitive stance toward his fellow employees. He believed they all wanted to avoid hard work, but that he could see through this and force good performances out of them. Clearly, he saw himself as an inherently hard worker and excellent performer, whose job it was to keep the lazy, incapable ones in line. No wonder his subordinates distrusted him and wanted to work somewhere else. No wonder his managerial peers saw him as aloof and self-centered. Actually, Bill saw himself as clearly superior to his peers and more deserving of a promotion.

In our continuing sessions, it became clear that Bill's inability to deepen relationships with coworkers extended to his family. Seeing his wife and children as self-indulgent and impulsive, he treated them essentially the same way he did his employees. Soon, his wife, feeling increasingly desperate and on the verge of separating from him, came in for counseling. It was clearly very painful for her to be on the receiving end of Bill's competitive interpersonal strategy. We tried to help his wife see how she could influence his behavior toward her and the children, without just escaping. We encouraged and assisted her in unilaterally giving him assistance and encouragement.

Through our ongoing, insight-oriented coaching of Bill, he began to see that the consequences of his actions in the workplace and at home were just the opposite of what was needed to achieve success. Instead of bringing the best out of his subordinates at work, he was making them bitter, disloyal, and dissatisfied, leading them to cut corners and sabotage. At home, he was courting divorce. He realized that what he really needed to do was the very opposite of his interactional strategy.

Specifically, he needed to compliment and reward people (rather than to ignore them) when they performed well and to help them (rather than to be critical and punitive) when their performance was not up to standard. The next step was for him to realize that, deep down, in his heart of hearts, he actually felt overwhelmed with stress and perilously weak, however much he professed the opposite. He desperately wanted the help of his subordinates and family members, and finally saw how he was paradoxically undermining any chance of getting their help.

He began to try to change, but it was too little, too late at that company. Unfortunately, he was fired. The upside of this, however, is that he made a new start at another company, where he had no damaging legacy to overcome. In the new job, his interactions with other employees were much better, reflecting what he had learned in hardiness training and how he had changed. He was able to give assistance and encouragement for the first time in his life. His subordinates worked hard for him and were loyal, and his peers and supervisors admired him. In effect, he was getting assistance and encouragement back from all of them. Furthermore, he and his family are still together and are making progress toward more loving, constructive relationships.

Now that you've read Bill's story, we want you to think carefully about your own interactions with people at work. Do any of the people involved in these interactions treat you as though they believe you are not interested in, or capable of, performing well? If so, they probably feel overwhelmed themselves and are blind to their part in damaging the relationship. It would certainly be understandable for you to retaliate angrily, or withdraw, but neither approach will improve the relationship. Fortunately, there is an alternative that may actually increase the closeness and comfort you feel toward coworkers. That alternative involves the exercises in chapter 10.

JULIE W.: "I LOVE BEING THE CENTER OF ATTENTION."

Although attractive and capable, Julie was forever comparing herself to those around her. She was an administrative assistant in the billing department of a large manufacturing company. Whenever she encountered people who looked striking or had something memorable to say, Julie would find something about them to criticize behind their backs. According to her, they didn't know as much as they thought they did, or they were just trying much too hard to impress people.

If Julie and her peers in the company were working together on a project, she would inevitably try to correct how they were performing, showing them her own, ostensibly better way. Usually, she would try to find what seemed a helpful way to change their actions but would become more strident if they did not acquiesce. These peers were simultaneously attracted to, and wary of, working with her. The problem would get exacerbated when there were disruptive, stressful changes in work routine, brought about by such things as computer advances or new customer needs. At times like these, all the employees would be struggling to change what they had been doing in order to address the new problems. It was hard on all of them, and this was worsened by Julie's even more strident insistence at those times that her way was the right way.

In her midtwenties, Julie lived alone, having had several relationships with men break up because she felt they were not good enough for her. The women who became Julie's friends were those who let her take the lead in whatever was going on. She decided what they would do, where they would go, what they would wear, and how it would turn out. Julie was the talker and the dresser among them, and they tended to lapse into passivity when she really got going. She liked to think of her tendency to dominate as a sign of her capability and leadership. But, when people would speak up, responding to something she said, Julie would just cut them off, continue talking as if she were the only person in the room, and fail to listen long enough to respond in a sensitive way.

When she was with just one or two of her friends or coworkers, Julie would subtly criticize those who were not present. "Did you notice how Jean was dressed the other day? It didn't seem so appropriate to what we were doing." Or, "Don't you wonder why Amanda is always letting the boss get the better of her? Maybe she just doesn't think well of herself." But, it wasn't just one or two of her friends that Julie would criticize. Every one of them was fair game, as long as he or she were not present to hear it.

However remarkable Julie's presentation of herself appeared, many people steered clear of her. This troubled her, even though she tended to see it as their limitation, not hers. Men, in particular, would be initially attracted to her looks and spirit, but rarely stayed involved once they got to know her better. At the office, fellow employees tended not to befriend her and tried to get their work done without her insistent "help."

Actually, she came to us for hardiness training, as the years went by with her feeling increasingly isolated, despite what she perceived as her efforts to help people do better. In her mind, the gathering gloom of a life alone was because there were no people available who could match her assertiveness and capability. She felt that, although the problem was theirs, she was stuck with the unacceptable outcome and wanted help in adjusting to that.

As her training progressed, Julie became better able to face the underlying problem. She had always felt personally inadequate and spent her life trying to overcome this sense of inferiority by struggling for convincing evidence that she was indeed better than she thought. This evidence took the form of showing herself that she could do things better than anyone else she encountered.

Gradually, through our coaching, Julie came to recognize this subtle competition in which she was constantly engaged. She began to realize that people who avoided her after being initially attracted were doing so because it is dissatisfying to be in a supposedly supportive relationship at work, to say nothing of romance, where you are constantly being one-upped. With this deeper, though painful, self-awareness, she was able to struggle to feel better about herself in other ways than in trying to prove those around her inferior.

■ She practiced listening to others, drawing them out, and moderating her attempt to aggrandize herself.

■ She tried to appreciate and facilitate effectiveness in others, rather than to feel threatened by it.

■ She changed her pattern of relationships to include people who would have seemed a threat to her in the past.

■ Her work relationships began to become more mutually cooperative and effective in reaching the department's goals.

Before long, Julie's company considered her for a promotion. She also found an interesting man to date and, soon, he became her fiancé.

Do you have a significant other who, like Julie, has to show up those around her, even work-team members, family members, or friends? Do you notice that, if someone else seems particularly remarkable or has performed really well, he or she feels belittled? If so, you will recognize that it is hard to let down your guard with him or her, so the relationship cannot really progress toward greater mutual effectiveness in reaching goals, to say nothing of greater fulfillment and intimacy. Once again, recognize that you have an alternative in your reaction to such a person, and the clue to this is the recognition of how stressed and inadequate he or she must feel.

And, here is a harder question: Do you recognize signs of subtle competition in yourself as you interact with your fellow employees, family members, and friends? If so, try to recognize your own sense of inadequacy that is fueling such ineffective behavior and substitute assistance and encouragement instead. In this way, your relationships will improve, and you will become a more effective person. The exercises in chapter 10 will get you started in helping others and yourself overcome subtle competition with coworkers, family, and friends.

JIM T.: "IF SOMEBODY HURTS ME, YOU CAN BE SURE I'LL GET BACK AT HIM."

In his midforties, Jim's marriage was ending badly. The divorce court judge had referred him to us for hardiness training. As he talked with us, he seemed so bitter about the world around him. He seemed to remember every time someone had hurt him and was resolved to get back at him one way or another. In his mind, it was a sign of weakness to let a slight go unpunished. These slights would fester in his mind, disrupt his concentration, and waste his imagination. They would keep him awake at night and undermine his ability to function effectively on mutual tasks, to say nothing about having fun and feeling fulfilled in his interaction with others.

Among his fellow employees, Jim had the reputation of being a difficult person to work with. If a coworker pointed out an error he had made or if there was a strong disagreement as to how to proceed on a task, Jim never forgot it and looked for some way to even the score. His engineering background made him indispensable on his work team, but the others got to the point of trying very hard to circumvent him, which only made him more difficult to deal with. Soon, the decision makers in his company were contemplating whether they should let him go, despite his intelligence and importance to his team. The message of "don't mess with me" was leading toward a "divorce" at work also.

From our sessions with Jim, we came to realize that he and his wife had many disagreements about what they wanted in their life together and how to get it. She had no trouble articulating her needs and wishes, and would occasionally veto his initiatives if they seemed inconsiderate. Jim tended to feel hurt when he could not do what he wanted and get her to join in. This hurt would turn into anger as he ruminated about and exaggerated the situation in his mind. Then, the anger would fester, leading him to strike back at her by automatically denying something she wanted from him. He would do this even if he liked what she wanted—so important was his need to even the score. The birth of children complicated his ability to build a mutually satisfying relationship. Being young, the children wanted what they wanted, when they wanted it, and this was sometimes inconsistent with Jim's sense of what he and the family should be doing. So, he would punish the kids for being insubordinate. The situation got worse, as his wife increasingly felt she had to divorce him for the children's sake as well as her own.

When he first talked to us about this divorce, he made it seem as if it were entirely his wife's fault. He remembered all those times when he wanted to go golfing or hiking or to the movies, but his wife backed out—it was always something with her, according to Jim, from feeling sick or tired, to being too busy with the kids.

He seemed so intent on paying her back for these frustrations, which he experienced as abandonment, that he failed to be there for her when she needed him and he curtailed her spending money on the grounds of sudden frugality. Sometimes, if their kids felt sick, his wife would draft him to stay home and minister to them, preventing him from engaging in some activity that would have been more fun. This would make him sullen and aloof around the house and lead him to insist that the kids stay home long after they felt better, with the excuse that "hey, if they're sick, they're sick."

Although more subtle, Jim's behavior was equally competitive at work. He secretly felt rejected and humiliated whenever his suggestions were not immediately accepted or his work was sent back for revision. In such situations, he would present himself as acceptant of the feedback, but try to ferret out who was responsible and resolve to get back at him. When some later work situation required his reaction, he would reject the initiatives or plans, whether they had merit or not. Jim was careful to hide his hurt and angry response, but the others increasingly avoided him, even though they could not put their finger on exactly why they reacted this way. As he became more and more isolated at work, his contribution to the overall effort of the company increasingly came into question.

Jim needed to work on his inability to give assistance and encouragement to his coworkers, friends, and family. If a significant other hurts you, it is more constructive to express the hurt, rather than to turn it into anger and strike back. Expressing the hurt is likely to provoke the other to recognize what he or she has done, apologize for or explain it, and try to do better. In contrast, expressing anger, even subtly, is likely to provoke a defensive or angry response that will only further undermine your ability to work or live together.

It took a lot of coaching for Jim to recognize his contribution to interactional difficulties. To achieve this recognition, he had to realize that, deep down, he felt inadequate and weak, and had been covering this up by convincing himself of the opposite. Unfortunately, by the time he gained these insights, his job and his marriage were long gone. Hopefully, he learned enough to put a more constructive effort into new jobs and relationships and to improve his relations with his children and former wife.

Does Jim's behavior sound all too familiar to you? Do you have friends or family who keep mental score pads as to who has hurt them and whether the necessary payback has occurred? Do they harbor resentment when interactions don't go just the way they want them to? Do they spend time thinking through how to get back at people? Now, think carefully, do you show any of these characteristics?

A "yes" to any of these questions means that you have experienced a lethal form of competition that undermines relationships and the ability to work with others, by insisting on an eye for an eye, and a tooth for a tooth, rather than on something more appreciative and patient. However hard it may be to react sensitively to subtle competition, try to recognize that, whether it is others or you who show it, underneath the facade of strength are feelings of weakness and vulnerability. The way to resolve subtle competition is with assistance and encouragement. The exercises in chapter 10 will help you interact in this way.

AMY S.: "THOSE WITH WHOM I WORK NEED ME TO PROTECT THEM, SO NOTHING BAD WILL EVER HAPPEN TO THEM."

In her late thirties, Amy was the manager of a small real estate firm and a wife and mother. Hopelessly busy, she was nonetheless a loving, caring person, committed to helping those around her. She came to us as consultants to help improve the performance of her subordinates at work.

Almost all of the six agents working under Amy were female and younger than she was. They seemed a close-knit group, with lots of sharing, not only of work tasks and information, but of personal matters as well. Amy brought us in primarily because she hoped to improve the overall effectiveness of the group, in particular, two agents she regarded as disruptive. As we observed the group in action, something became abundantly clear: Amy was a micromanager. She simply did not feel comfortable letting the agents carry out their tasks using their own knowledge, imagination, and persistence.

Amy had started this company, and therefore felt she knew not only how it should function, but how to make that happen. She involved herself in all the ongoing decisions, no matter how much time it took. All of the agents felt that Amy did not trust them to function on their own, and four of them had chosen to accept that. They let her make all the decisions, big and small, and merely followed her instructions. As time went on, however, Amy began to wonder why they seemed to have so little imagination and initiative.

Two of the agents were less willing to let her make all the decisions and kept trying to be independent in their work efforts. These two seemed to Amy to be on the verge of insubordination and a threat to the rest of the company. Amy couldn't understand why they wouldn't let her help them more.

As we talked with Amy about the problem, she expressed feeling like the agents were her children. She felt she needed to take care of them, protect them from outside pressures and from making mistakes, and help them be successful. It was a novel idea to her when we wondered whether, by being overprotective, she might be stifling their creativity and initiative, and increasing their resentment. In her mind, she wanted only the best for them and the company. But, she listened to us, because she did want to do the best thing for everybody.

In our training sessions with Amy, she began to reflect on whether she showed the same overprotective pattern with her actual children. She recounted a recent series of events involving her thirteen-year-old son. He came home from school crying one day because two of his friends had suddenly decided to shun him and go off by themselves. He felt rejected by people he had befriended.

Amy felt so bad for her son that, unbeknownst to him, she called the parents of the two boys, complaining about what had taken place. She asked the parents to talk to their sons about being more civil and accepting of her boy. The next afternoon, her son came home from school crying even more profusely, and quite angry at his mother, vowing not to share problems with her in the future. Having been admonished by their parents, his erstwhile friends had ridiculed him to all the other students as a wimp who couldn't fight his own battles and needed to hide behind his mother's apron strings.

Amy had wondered at the time whether she had done something wrong, despite her efforts to help the boy she loved to have a better life. Now, as she discussed this event with us in the context of overprotection, she began to realize that it would have been better for her to empathize with and encourage her son that first day and refrain from trying to settle the problem with the other parents. After all, no laws had been broken, and there was no reason to believe that her son could not have coped with the situation, especially with her loving support.

When we overprotect others, we indirectly convey that we distrust their ability to solve problems effectively, and that, to survive, they need us to assist and protect them. If they accept the overprotection, then they are agreeing that they are not effective in the situation, and this will undermine their capability in the future. That's what happened to Amy's four agents. If they reject our overprotection, then they may confront us with direct or subtle anger, and the relationship may suffer in the process. That's what happened to Amy's other two agents. In neither case does overprotection enhance overall effectiveness and build trust and understanding. However loving we may feel toward significant others, it is a mistake to overprotect them. It is better for everyone to give and receive assistance and encouragement.

Did Amy's plight provoke you to notice overprotectiveness expressed toward you? Or, do you suspect that you overprotect the significant others around you? If so, you want to take the exercises in chapter 10 very seriously.

WHERE DO YOU FIT IN?

Take a few minutes to answer the following questions as "True" or "False" in order to get a concrete sense of how you interact with your coworkers, now and in the past. Remember, no one will see your answers but you, so be as honest as you can.

HIGH IN SOCIAL SUPPORT

1. When coworkers are stressed by workplace changes, do you express your sympathy and try to draw them out?

2. When coworkers are stressed about workplace changes, do you try to help them find ways of dealing with the problems that work for them?

3. When you are stressed out by workplace changes, do you seek out coworkers to talk with about the problems?

4. When you stress out about workplace changes, do you ask coworkers for their suggestions?

5. Do you see your company and yourself as trying to grow and do better?

6. Do you feel you and your coworkers make a team effort to carry out work goals?

LOW IN SOCIAL SUPPORT

1. When interacting with coworkers on job tasks, do you withhold information that would enhance their learning or advancement?

2. When interacting with coworkers on job tasks, do you take over any problem that isn't routine, in order to ensure that they will not mess it up?

3. In order to stop coworkers from getting ahead, do you complain about them to management?

4. Do you feel relieved when someone at work takes over a problem, so that you don't have to deal with it?

5. Does it seem naive to you to think of the work environment as anything but a dog-eat-dog world?

6. Do you tend to stay aloof from others at work, in order to protect yourself against possible attempts to undermine you?

To score your answers, give yourself one point for each time you answered "True" to a question. In order to see your social interaction approach, total your scores for each set of six questions. Did you score high or low in Social Support? Keep these results in mind as you read further.

SUMMARY

The bottom line is that competition (whether subtle or obvious) and overprotection have paradoxical effects. Even if we have difficulty enlisting the support of others, we should still do what we can to assist and encourage them. This increases the likelihood that they will reciprocate these efforts. Relationships of mutual assistance and encouragement bring the best out of all parties, and in ways that are especially important when stressful changes need to be turned to advantage. The feedback you will receive from this constructive process will help to deepen your hardy attitudes of commitment, control, and challenge. With this enhanced courage and motivation, the whole process of interacting in a way that elicits social support will become easier and more natural. The result will be a marked increase in your own resiliency as well as that of your coworkers, friends, and family.

CHAPTER 10

PRACTICING SOCIALLY SUPPORTIVE INTERACTIONS

You support people in a resilient way by creating relationships that are effective, satisfying, and intimate. You can accomplish this even when the relationship involves healthy goal-striving or mentoring. In consistent patterns of destructive competition and overprotection, however, supportive connections break down. This undermines all parties, and if unchanged through supportive actions like assistance and encouragement, relationships take a downward turn. Forming supportive work relationships is more doable than it may sound, and the effort is more than worth it. Resiliency is positively connected to employee and employer effectiveness through its link to citizenship behavior.[1]

Let's start by considering what makes someone a "significant other." At work, your significant others are the people you interact with regularly in order to get tasks done. This certainly includes your team members, supervisors, and supervisees. Depending on the company organization, it may also include fellow committee members, consulting experts, and even peers, if you and they influence each other. The defining characteristic of a significant relationship is that you and the person regularly influence each other's performance effectiveness, self-worth, self-definition, and sense of common cause in the company.

Outside of work, but often relevant to it, are your immediate family members, and even less immediate ones, if you interact with them regularly in a way that influences your functioning. Also relevant are your close friends and perhaps an occasional fellow member of organizations important to you, like religious congregations and community groups. Social relationships outside of work affect our performance and health. Therefore, we must consider our influence on the self-definition, worth, and performance of fellow coworkers, friends, and family, as well as their influences on us.

You are definitely fortunate if you and your significant others are already exchanging assistance and encouragement, without any further effort on your part. But, if your relationships are characterized by competition or overprotection, you will have to initiate the steps toward resolving the existing conflicts. If you take the initiative, this greatly increases the probability that the other people will join in constructively. It does not help to point out insistently everything that other people are doing wrong, however valid this may seem. This kind of critical confrontation, even if accurate, will engender defensiveness in them, defensiveness that may actually worsen the situation. Then, you will get into a never-ending spiral of stressful criticisms, without much good coming of it. Of course, someone can always decide to end the relationship. But, for coworkers this may have negative consequences and for family members, devastating ones. As we have said before, the form of assertiveness that is best for fostering trust, cooperation, respect, and closeness in relationships that are problematic is more unilateral disarmament than attack.

In order to help you build resilience at work (and outside of work) through social support, we present here a three-step plan that encourages you to examine your relationships, to develop a way of solving the conflicts in these relationships, and to put your plan into action, one relationship at a time.

STEP ONE
CREATE A SOCIAL INTERACTION MAP

Write down the names of all the individuals who, through the roles you play in each other's lives, are important to you. Your map will certainly include your fellow employees with whom you must interact in order to get the company's work done. It will also include your immediate family members. There may also be other people, such as friends and more-remote family members, on your map.

Then, for each person on your list, indicate what it is that brings you into contact and what defines your relationship. You can do this by answering the following questions and specifying the connection between you as completely as you can. In answering these questions, you are recording for yourself the degree to which the people on your list are significant to you.

IDENTIFYING SIGNIFICANT OTHERS IN YOUR LIFE

In the case of fellow employees:

1. Are you in the same team or department?

2. Is the person your supervisor?

3. Is the person your supervisee?

4. Does the person have a consulting function for you (such as legal or computer expert)?

5. Are there also more informal connections between you (such as sharing church membership or having regular lunches together)?

In the case of family members:

1. Is the person your spouse or child?

2. Is the person your parent or sibling?

3. Is the person a more distant relation, such as your uncle, aunt, or cousin?

4. Is the person related to you by blood?

5. Do you live in the same home as the person?

6. Do you meet with the person regularly?

7. Do you have only occasional contact, such as by telephone or at celebrations?

In the case of friends or fellow members of organizations:

1. Is the relationship emotionally intimate?

2. Is the relationship physically intimate?

3. Do you interact with this person every day?

4. Do you interact with this person regularly, yet not every day?

5. Do you interact with this person only occasionally?

6. Do you interact with this person only sporadically?

You now have the personal information to see just how close each person on your list comes to being a significant other in your life. As to fellow employees, if your job requires that you work together, they qualify as significant others. If you supplement work requirements with additional interaction, this intensifies the tie between you. For family members and friends, if you live together, you qualify as significant others. Once again, if you supplement the living arrangements with regular, intimate interactions, this also intensifies the tie between you.

Do Your Relationships Involve Conflict?

How well our lives progress is importantly influenced by how supportive the ongoing relationships are with the people we are close to. Now that you have clearly identified these people, you are ready for an additional, important process of reflection. Specifically, you need to recognize whether there is conflict in the relationship between you and each of your significant others.

Please be as discerning and honest as you can in answering the questions that follow, as your insights and conclusions are crucial in the attempt to improve your relationships. It will be helpful to you, in answering the questions, to keep in mind the insights and reflections you had while reading the examples of competition and overprotection included in chapter 9. Answer these specific questions with regard to your interaction pattern with the significant people in your life.

1. Does the person compete with you on the tasks to be performed?

2. Do you compete with the person on the tasks to be performed?

3. Does the person compete with you in interactions with others?

4. Do you compete with the person in interactions with others?

5. Does the person overprotect you on the tasks to be performed?

6. Do you overprotect the person on the tasks to be performed?

7. Does the person overprotect you in interactions with others?

8. Do you overprotect the person in interactions with others?

Answering these questions may be painful, especially when they show how you initiate interactions with the others. But, giving your best effort in answering will help you understand the specifics of conflicts you may be having with these people. Most conflicts arise from competition or overprotection. So, your observations here are a vital first step in the process of trying to resolve the conflicts.

You will emerge from this first step as having identified which of your relationships are conflicted, and whether the conflicts are the result of something you are doing, of something the other person is doing, or of some mutual contribution.

STEP TWO
SOLVING CONFLICTS THROUGH
ASSISTANCE AND ENCOURAGEMENT

You are definitely fortunate if some of your relationships are without continuing conflict and already involve a pattern of giving and receiving assistance and encouragement. But, when competition or overprotection characterizes a relationship with a significant other, you will have to initiate the changes that lead to resolving the conflict and replacing it with assistance and encouragement. If you initiate in this way, it will greatly increase the probability that the other person will join in constructively.

By now you have made a list of which of your relationships are mired in conflict. Select one of these relationships to work on in this second step. Some of our trainees prefer to choose a less central, less conflicted relationship, because that seems easier and permits greater concentration on the specifics of planning and taking needed actions. But, other trainees want to get going immediately on the most problematic and central relationships, the quicker to improve their life pattern. It's up to you which relationship you work on first. And, of course, once you have successfully worked on the first conflicted relationship, you will be going on to the next, and the next, until your list is complete.

UNDERSTANDING RELATIONSHIP CONFLICT

Resolving relationship conflict involves talking honestly and fully about the problem, and trying to behave more constructively. In order to be able to talk honestly and fully, you must reflect on the contributions both parties make to the problem and the debilitating effects of those contributions. To be really helpful to the other person in this process, you must look beyond the obvious, but do not do this with an ax to grind, even if you are feeling hurt and angry.

As if this were not hard enough, we are also asking you to reflect on whether you have actually been the instigating problem in the relationship. For most of us, this is a very difficult thing to admit, but makes all the difference in whether or not you can improve the relationship.

Answering the following questions will help you in this difficult process:

Question 1: Which of the following descriptions best characterizes your conflicted relationship?

- Both you and the other person keep trying to compete with each other. Describe how this happens. In doing this, keep in mind all you have read up to this point on ways in which competition gets expressed in relationships. You may find it especially helpful to recall the discussion of Bill F., Julie W., and Jim T. in chapter 9. In being as honest as you can about yourself, recognize that in some relationships, it's common for people to compete.

- Both you and the other person keep trying to overprotect each other. Describe how this happens. Be as honest as you can, keeping in mind all you have read on overprotection. It may be helpful to recall the story of Amy in chapter 9.

- The other person competes or overprotects, and you react defensively. Describe how this happens. In addition to detailing the other person's destructive ways, make sure to include how your reactions may be further undermining the relationship. In particular, do you withdraw or express angry criticism? Both of these reactions have an undermining effect, however understandable they may have seemed to you. Withdrawal and criticism will only engender even more defensiveness in the other person and are therefore inconsistent with the significant nature of the relationship.

- You compete or overprotect, and the other person reacts defensively. Describe how this happens. In addition to admitting your destructive ways, include how the other person's reactions are further undermining the relationship. Does he or she withdraw or express angry criticism? Once again, both of these reactions just make matters worse.

Question 2: In the conflicted relationship, what are the underlying feelings you and the other person are having?

The clue here is to get behind whatever you or the other person are saying and doing in order to find the underlying feelings.

Let's talk about competition first. What are the feelings behind this? Down deep, people who characteristically compete with significant others almost always feel inadequate in some way, and therefore envious. It's as if someone were saying, "Poor me, I'm not as capable (or as attractive) as he is." But, instead of accepting and admitting that, he denies it and slips into envy and competition. Blaming it on the other person, he'll say, "Who does he think he is? I'll show him who's best." If a significant other keeps competing with you, some of this must be going on. And, if you keep competing with him or her, you must be having these underlying feelings as well.

Something surprisingly similar happens in the case of overprotection. Troubled by underlying feelings of personal inadequacy, the overprotective person covers up these feelings by acting as if the opposite were true. This takes the form of belittling the capabilities of significant others and taking on responsibility for ensuring their safety and success. It's as if the overprotecting person were saying, "I'm not the inadequate one—she is. It's my job, therefore, to protect her from harm." If a significant other keeps overprotecting you, some of this must be going on. And, if you keep overprotecting her, you must be having these underlying feelings as well.

Now, let's focus on what it feels like to be on the receiving end of competition by a significant other. You don't see yourself as expressing competitiveness, but being the recipient of it. In this case, you are likely to feel hurt. You may think, "Why am I being treated this way? We are obviously not as close and cooperative as I thought. It makes me really sad." An aspect of this sense of hurt might even be to wonder whether you have done something or been weak in some way that encouraged the competition. "Maybe I'm just too naive and trusting," you may wonder. But, feelings of hurt often give way quickly to anger. You may ask yourself, "Who does she think she is?" or "There's no way she is going to get away with how I'm being treated." The reactions of hurt and anger tend to go together.

Once again, the feelings you have when someone is being overprotective of you are surprisingly similar to the feelings you have when someone is being competitive toward you. It is, of course, possible that you feel so overwhelmed and undermined that you welcome overprotection. More typically, however, when you interact with significant others, you expect some level of equality, or at least some recognition of it. When a significant other consistently overprotects you, it is likely to stimulate your feelings of hurt and anger. You may express such thoughts as, "Am I really as inadequate as he thinks I am?" The anger inheres in such reflections as, "Who is he to lord it over me as if I can't do anything successfully?" And, once again, the reactions of hurt and anger tend to go together.

It is important for you to be clear about the combination of feelings you and your significant other are having in the conflicted relationship that you want to improve. You both may be feeling anger, hurt, or personal unworthiness in various combinations and degrees, depending on whether you are the one being competitive or overprotective, or are on the receiving end of these behaviors, or something of both. Answering the next question will help you figure out how to express these feelings and address the feelings of your significant other in a manner that will help resolve the relational conflict.

Question 3: When you and your significant other are interacting and painful feelings are involved, what are the strengths and weaknesses of your communication styles?

The major difficulty with interactions that involve painful feelings is that we may act them out in ways that just make matters worse. Acting out these painful feelings is likely to lead to defensiveness on the part of the other person, and before you know it, the relationship has deteriorated further.

Let's say you are angry at a competitive coworker and say, "Who do you think you are? I can't even talk to you, because you always have to trump me." The defensive response to this is likely to be something like, "I don't know what you're talking about. I didn't try to hurt you." In return, you step up your anger, saying "You're weaseling out of it. I don't believe you didn't know what you were doing." Before you know it, the relationship will worsen, rather than improve. And, the scenario will be similar if you are the one being aggressively confronted by a significant other who feels you have competed incessantly with him or her.

Let's say you are being constantly overprotected by a family member and act out on your feelings of being seen as too inadequate to survive well. You might say, "You must think I'm such a wimp. Why don't you respect my capabilities? You're not the only one who can do well." Your family member may well respond defensively to this, saying, "Don't you know how much I care about your well-being? I'm just trying to protect you. But, I guess you don't see that." And this ticks you off even more as you say, "I don't need you to protect me. You must think you're God Almighty." This relationship is getting worse right before your eyes. And, the scenario is similar if you are the one being overprotective and are confronted aggressively by a family member.

COMMUNICATING CONSTRUCTIVELY

So, how is it possible to discuss conflicted interactions with a significant other in a way that can improve the relationship? Essentially, you must be aware of your feelings in the situation, but not act them out in a confrontational, critical manner. Instead, you need to talk about your painful feelings and those of your significant other, using that as a springboard to more constructive interaction. How can you do this?

Let's say that your coworker has been competing with you. In talking with him about this, you may say, "I've been feeling sad lately about our relationship. I know you don't mean to hurt me, but that's what happens when it seems to me like you want to get ahead. Part of the reason I feel hurt is because our relationship is so important to me. I'd like us to work in cooperation for the good of us both and what we have to accomplish." This form of communication is less likely to engender a defensive reaction from your coworker. Instead, he may say, "I'm sorry. I didn't know you were feeling bad about working with me. I was just trying to do my best. Yes, let's try to find a way to work together more."

A similar scenario may take place if it was you doing the competing, and your coworker wanted less conflict. If your coworker approached you in the way suggested above, you might also respond nondefensively.

Something equally constructive could result if the problem is chronic overprotection. In talking with a family member who is overprotective, you can make it clear you know she is trying to help you and this help is appreciated, but that it is hard for you to make contributions under these circumstances. If this is not done in an angry, blaming fashion, it increases the likelihood that the family member will not become defensive. She may even apologize and agree to find a way to work more constructively together. And, of course, if you are the overprotective one and your family member approaches you in the same way, this leads to positive effects as long as you remain open.

In coming up with your answer to Question 3, think through the specific feelings involved in the conflicted relationship you are working on and see if you can imagine having a calm, mutually appreciative discussion of the problem. Can you see yourself approaching the significant other in the manner we have suggested here? If so, that may make all the difference in the world. For you and your significant other, it may pave the way for a pattern of giving and receiving assistance and encouragement.

BUILDING A PATTERN OF ENCOURAGEMENT AND ASSISTANCE

In order to be able to build two-way assistance and encouragement into a hitherto-conflicted relationship with a significant other, you must transcend your painful feelings of hurt, anger, and inadequacy so that you can work on reaching potentials, rather than being bogged down in actualities. Initiating the constructive dialogue emphasized above is a major step toward socially supportive interactions. Once that dialogue is underway, it is time for you to begin giving assistance and encouragement to your significant other. If this has to start as a sole contribution on your part, so be it. When the significant other receives assistance and encouragement from you, it will be hard for him or her not to give it back.

Let us refresh your memory about the meaning of assistance and encouragement. To encourage significant others, you must first be empathetic toward them. This involves being able to put yourself in their shoes, to experience life and its stress the way they do. Empathy leads to being sympathetic, to wishing to facilitate their struggles to meet goals, perform effectively, and feel fulfillment. The final aspect of encouragement is feeling and expressing confidence in, and admiration for, the significant others.

In summary, when significant others experience stressful circumstances, you appreciate their dilemmas, want the best for them, and believe in them enough to think they will be successful. As you can see, this is not at all the same as wanting to compete with them. Nor is it the same as overprotecting them, though the distinction here is more subtle.

Overprotection means not wanting significant others to experience any painful feelings or stressful circumstances, regardless of whether going through that process is inevitable in order for them to reach their goals and to develop. In contrast, encouragement is being supportive and facilitative, but accepting the life trajectory your significant others have chosen as important and worthwhile, and believing them capable of succeeding in it. We hope you see this difference, as it is very important.

Assisting significant others is more concrete, but needs to build on your wish to encourage them. Specifically, in assisting, you are willing to do whatever you can to facilitate them in their efforts to cope effectively with the stressful circumstances they experience. There are three general ways of doing this:

1. One involves *contributing your resources* to facilitate the efforts being made by your significant others. If you have some knowledge or expertise that will help them, you give it willingly. If you have some contacts that can provide the knowledge or expertise that will help, you make them available. If you are a good sounding board, you offer that as a way to facilitate their planning.

2. Another way is by *taking up the slack*. If your significant others are preoccupied by their struggle to cope with stressful circumstances, you may temporarily take over some of their responsibilities that are not directly relevant to that particular struggle.

3. Related to this is yet another way of assisting significant oth-
    ers that *gives them space they need* if they are attempting to
    cope with stressful circumstances. Perhaps they are so over-
    whelmed that they are not giving you the usual level of atten-
    tion and interaction your relationship enjoys. You can assist
    them by simply accepting this temporary distance, without
    reacting negatively to it as unwarranted rejection.

In summary, you can assist by making your expertise and contacts available, temporarily accepting uncharacteristic distance,
and taking over nonessential tasks. You don't want to make this
assistance on your part a permanent feature of the relationship.
Rather, it is a constructive response when your significant other is
temporarily preoccupied with the struggle to cope with stressful
changes.

This assistance is not at all the same as being competitive. The
distinction between assistance and overprotection is more subtle,
but hardly unimportant. In assisting, you are not taking over the
person's tasks and efforts. Instead, you are facilitating his or her
efforts. That person is still the decision maker and initiator with
regard to the stressful circumstances that impinge and need resolution.

To be sure, our emphasis in the preceding paragraphs is for
you and others to give unilateral assistance and encouragement.
Some may feel like this is giving in. If you do this, however, with
hardy attitudes, these interactions will strengthen you. Remember,
by the time you give assistance and encouragement, you will already have initiated a discussion of the relationship conflict and
how it might be resolved. And, you will communicate that you
will start giving assistance and encouragement, and hope, in turn,
to receive it back. Under these circumstances, it is very difficult
for someone profiting from assistance and encouragement not to
give it back. The aim is to initiate the process of improving the
relationship. With regard to this process, you must consider two
key questions.

Question 1: Specifically, how will you offer encouragement to your significant other?

It is time to become more specific about the particular relationship you are trying to improve. In particular, how will you offer encouragement as your significant other attempts to struggle with stressful circumstances?

Building on the insight you have gained through answering previous questions, you may well be able to sense the specifics of what it is like to be in the other person's shoes. Elaborate this empathic observation for yourself. Once you feel what he or she must be feeling, use that as a basis for constructing a sympathetic communication. Be specific about what you will say that is sympathetic enough to convince the other person that you really sense what he or she is going through.

Having gone that far, reflect on ways in which you consider the significant other capable and able to be effective. Further, what are the ways in which you admire him or her? In order to go through this process of reflection well, you will, of course, have to put the feelings of hurt and anger you were having behind you. Hopefully, you have accomplished this already in finding answers to previous questions in this social support process. Keep trying, as it is time now for you to find words that convey your support of and admiration for the significant other, even though your relationship has involved some conflict up to now.

Question 2: Specifically, how will you offer assistance to your significant other?

Here, too, your task is to become as specific as you can about particular ways in which you will offer assistance. Having identified the steps your significant other is trying to take to cope with or solve the problems created by stressful circumstances, you need to ask yourself what you can do that will help him or her in this process. Remember the three aspects of assistance.

Does it make sense to give the person some space? If so, then how? Perhaps you can encourage him or her not to attend the next routine department meeting or two in order to save time and energy for the coping effort.

Is it useful temporarily to take on some of his or her tasks that are less relevant to the stressful circumstance? If so, which tasks, and how will you perform them? Perhaps you can answer the person's routine customer requests over the next few days, when the bulk of the effort to cope with the stressful change needs to take place.

Are there specific resources you possess or that are available to you that would help the person's efforts? If so, what are they and how can they be accessed? Perhaps you have dealt with this kind of stressor before and have accumulated knowledge of what tends to work, and what does not. Or, perhaps you have a friend in another company with this kind of information and can introduce your significant other to him or her.

STEP THREE
CARRY OUT YOUR ACTION PLAN AND PAY ATTENTION TO THE FEEDBACK YOU GET

By now, you have done a lot of work leading up to an Action Plan aimed at increasing the social support in your conflicted relationship. Specifically, you have planned to start communicating in a way that transcends your painful feelings resulting from the conflict and emphasizes how the relationship can improve. Further, you have planned how to communicate about and act on giving assistance and encouragement unilaterally, so that your significant other can better cope with the ongoing stressful circumstances. It is time, now, for you to be very specific about your plan and how you will carry it out.

Question 1: What is the content of your Action Plan?

You are ready now to write down the specifics of what you want to accomplish by communicating with your significant other about improving your relationship. As we have already covered, you want to flag the problems of your interaction pattern, and try to replace them with assistance and encouragement instead. You want to say that you will try to give assistance and encouragement whenever necessary, rather than insist that your significant other do that for you. These are the abstract goals you are trying to reach.

But, what you need to specify here in order to make your Action Plan particularly relevant are the specifics of what you will try to communicate. What will determine these specifics is the particular nature of the relationship that makes you significant for each other. For example, are you the supervisee, the supervisor, or are you a peer? Are you the person who has been competing or over-protecting, or is it the significant other? Such considerations will influence how you try to communicate about initiating improvements. The questions you have already answered in Step One of this chapter will certainly help you in identifying and working within the particular nature of your relationship as you communicate.

Question 2: What are the logistics of your Action Plan?

In formulating your Action Plan, make sure to include the logistical opportunities and limitations imposed on your communication by the particular nature of the relationship. Assuming that the other person is significant for you because you work together, you need to consider how the two of you are likely to be able to talk with each other. One convenient venue is to plan regular private meetings together, especially if it is group meetings that you are accustomed to. If meetings are not common, you can ask for them. Or, perhaps there are occasional, informal encounters, such as meetings in the lunchroom, that would be helpful. You are, of course, looking for venues that are private, given the nature of the communication you plan.

Try to utilize regularly occurring meetings that are private enough to permit you to raise the topic of your relationship and how to improve it. If there are none, then try to find a way of initiating a meeting that is appropriate under your circumstances. In particular, your first meeting concerning how to improve the relationship needs to be private. After all, your significant other may be surprised by your expression of concern and wish to improve things.

Once that meeting takes place, you can go ahead and take steps to give assistance and encouragement, assuming that he or she will recognize those efforts as what you said you were going to do. But, it is useful to arrange subsequent meetings from time to time so that you can get feedback on your initial efforts. These subsequent meetings will also have the effect, along with your ongoing efforts to help, of increasing the likelihood that your significant other will be reciprocating with assistance and encouragement for you. Remember, building resiliency through social support is a two-way street.

REVISING YOUR ACTION PLAN

The specifics of your Action Plan may need revision periodically. After all, the magnitude, frequency, and accumulation of stressful circumstances may change over time for you and your significant other. When your significant other is overwhelmed, you need to intensify your efforts toward assistance and encouragement. And, the same is true for him or her when you are overwhelmed. It is also true that some of your specific efforts to give assistance and encouragement may work better than others with this particular significant other. Your observations of this may help you to refine or modify your Action Plan to ensure it is working as well as possible.

THREE SOURCES OF FEEDBACK ON SOCIAL SUPPORT

Remember the three sources of feedback to your transformational coping efforts (see chapter 7) that are important in building up your hardy attitudes? Well, the same three are relevant here in connection with your social support efforts. Specifically, there are observations (1) that you make of yourself, (2) that others make of you, and (3) that involve the intended effects of your efforts.

Imagine how much better you will feel when you observe yourself actually taking steps to improve your problematic relationship with a significant other, not detaching or reacting out of anger and self-pity. You might say, "Is that me? I didn't know I could do that. Maybe I can turn my life around more than I thought!"

And, wouldn't it be great if the people around you give you positive feedback on your efforts? They might say, "Boy, I didn't think you had the guts to try to make these changes. We all gave up long ago, but now we think you may be on the right track."

Also important will be the feedback you get from the reactions of the significant other who is the object of your efforts. You will see that when you give the precious gifts of assistance and encouragement, it is very hard for the other person not to value them and act similarly in return. Before you know it, you will have improved the relationship, and you will both be more effective on the tasks you work on together. Your significant other will be very appreciative. And, you will turn to each other when you have need.

All this positive feedback will deepen your hardy attitudes, making you more enthusiastic and forward-looking about your life, and more able to be courageous and motivated about finding fulfillment despite stressful circumstances. In short, you will be more resilient. Remember the two people we discussed at the beginning of chapter 9 who were suffering the debilitating effects of a lack of social support at work without even realizing it? Let's revisit them here.

DAVID G.: "I'M SO GLAD I FINALLY REALIZED
THAT TEAM MEMBERS CAN ACTUALLY
WORK TOGETHER."

Through his hardiness training, David began to realize that his anxiety and tension at work expressed the contradiction between the expectation that his team members would work together, and their insistent competitiveness with each other. Once he recognized this conflict, the training exercises helped him to consider what he might do to get his coworkers to work together. After careful deliberation, he came up with an Action Plan.

The first step in David's Action Plan involved taking the initiative in helping his coworkers to see their competitive ways and recognize how this undermined the effectiveness of the whole team. He raised this problem at lunches with the team members he thought would be most likely to respond positively. After they agreed with his analysis, he then took his message to the regularly scheduled team meetings. What he advocated was that the team as a whole would do better and reach its goals faster if everyone helped each other. And, this improvement in reaching work goals would make them all look good with the company, in addition to helping them to feel safe in working together. The others generally reacted positively to his message, though it was initially hard for them to give up being wary of each other.

The second step in David's Action Plan was to start unilaterally giving assistance and encouragement to team members. This was hard at first, as he felt especially vulnerable. But, before long, team members started trying to react in kind to him, to help with his work efforts. He kept making sure they all shared their observations of each other's efforts, both in informal meetings and in regular team sessions. As time went on, not only did they all feel safer and closer with each other, but it became apparent to all in the company that the team was reaching its assigned goals faster and more effectively. And, of course, David has long since stopped feeling anxiety and tension, and instead is enthusiastic about and capable in his work.

JANE W.: "MY BOSS MEANT WELL, BUT NEEDED TO LET ME DEVELOP MORE."

Hardiness training helped Jane realize that her feelings of boredom and stultification were primarily the result of her boss overprotecting her. He micromanaged to the point where all there was for her to do was follow directions routinely. As a result, she felt irrelevant, and thought her career was going nowhere. But, as she analyzed the situation further, she realized that her boss meant well, though he was too worried and threatened about outcomes to give anyone else a chance to perform. With this important insight, her mood shifted from pain and anger toward him, to pity and concern for him. At this point, she was ready to formulate an Action Plan.

The first step of Jane's Action Plan involved talking with her boss about the problem. She invited him to lunch, and focused first on how hard it must be for him to shoulder the enormous pressure of the high goals imposed on his department by the company. She also hastened to assure him that she saw him as very capable, despite the pressure. He responded gratefully to her observations.

Then, she let him know that she really wanted to help

more than her role permitted, emphasizing that this not only would be advantageous to him, but would also give her a greater sense of purpose and commitment to the department. She wondered whether he would feel OK about giving her a greater role in the work, so that they could both feel better. This was hard for him to hear, but he was impressed with her observations and initiative. They resolved to have lunch on a regular basis, to discuss their interaction further.

As the second step of her Action Plan, Jane began to give active encouragement and support to her boss. Soon, he was reacting positively toward her, almost as a friend. He opened up more and more about his worries at work, and this gave her an opportunity to give assistance, in the form of suggestions and commitments to take on various tasks. She was careful not to usurp his authority and judgment, so that he would not feel threatened.

As time went on, he started giving her tasks to carry out without his manipulative control. Soon, he was giving her assistance and encouragement in carrying out these tasks. Their relationship improved greatly, she no longer felt stultified, and he saw her as a valuable colleague. Down the road, she actually got a promotion, which her boss supported. Although this made her very happy, the one downside of it was that they missed working together.

SUMMARY

So far, you have worked on improving one of the problematic relationships on your list. Once you have begun to be successful in turning that first relationship around, pick another from your list and work on that as well, using the same tools presented in this chapter. And, as that second relationship begins to improve, add the third. Keep the processes going, until you improve the various conflicted relationships that you have with others.

What a difference this will make in your life! As time goes on, you will feel more and more social support. This in turn will make it much easier to throw yourself into transformational coping, or solving the problems constituted by stressful changes you encounter by turning them from potential disasters into opportunities. Soon, you will have all the courage and resiliency skills you need for success in the twenty-first century, a time of unprecedented change.

CHAPTER 11

STRENGTHENING EMPLOYEE AND EMPLOYER TIES

"Never work just for money or power.
They don't save your soul or help you sleep at night."
—MARIAN WRIGHT EDELMAN[1]

To thrive in these turbulent, changing times, both employees and employers need agendas that correspond to each other in realizing their mutual potential. This may be difficult, considering today's economic realities. But, just "staying above water" does not assure companies will thrive in rapidly changing, technologically innovative marketplaces. To thrive, companies and their employees must continually adapt and resiliently search out the potential opportunities within ongoing changes.

While employee and employer share the objective of avoiding the possible downward economic pressures inherent in changes, they may differ as to how to bring this about. Approaching changes by carving out new directions, and all that is involved in this, will consume the energy and focus of companies. But, in this attempt to thrive, a company needs its workforce to jump on board of its organizational initiatives for change. The best way for companies to accomplish this is by infusing their organizations' procedures and policies with resiliency (see chapter 12). Here, we concern ourselves with how individuals can strengthen ties to their companies while at the same time thriving on change.

Most employees try to carry out company policies and procedures. But they vary in their resilience to do so. When their resilience is high, employees readily endorse and adopt company changes. But, when their resilience is low, employees may only stay on board for the job security and income. A recent Gallup poll points to a dangerous situation concerning the U.S. workforce. The results show that 55 percent of the workforce are not engaged in their work, and another 19 percent are actively disengaged. Only 25 percent actually feel engaged.[2]

Juxtapose these poll figures with the results of several other surveys showing that today's employees value meaningful work and job satisfaction over income.[3] While income certainly pays the bills, it does not "save your soul or help you sleep at night." Human beings need meaningful work to thrive.[4] When you like what you do each day, you are apt to draw on skills and talents that express your nature, even in doing the most seemingly unimportant tasks. Human beings have the unique ability to utilize activities, like work, for creative expression and fulfillment of life purpose and meaning. Unfulfilling work stifles these human capacities.

One answer to the problem of feeling disengaged at work is to build up your individual hardiness. Hardiness will make you more resilient and more apt to find meaning in stressful changes and to derive benefits from these changes.[5] When you let circumstances deprive your life and work of meaning, you become depressed, angry, hopeless, and apathetic.

THREE WAYS TO FIND MEANING IN YOUR WORK

1. DEVELOP STRONG WORK RELATIONSHIPS. One opportunity to find meaning in what you do each day is to nurture your work relationships so that you feel socially satisfied as a member of a team. A strong work network buffers you against the more painful aspects of your daily work tasks. Think about your work experience. Did you ever stay long at a company in which you disliked coworkers and management? Were you more comfortable in jobs when you had strong work relationships?

Employees' complaints normally concern personal conflict with coworkers or a supervisor, not work-task problems. And, when employees sue their employers, it's most often when they feel personally maltreated by coworkers or management. It's amazing how much stress a person can endure if it occurs in the context of a socially satisfying work environment. The quality of your work relationships strongly influences how meaningful work is to you. When you and your coworkers commit to supporting each other's productivity and satisfaction, the work environment is a nicer place to be.

2. LOOK AT THE BIG PICTURE. Seeing how your job fits into a larger organizational context provides another opportunity to find meaning in your work. If you learn more about your company's various department functions and procedures, you connect more deeply to the company as a whole. You see your contributions to the workplace as more meaningful when you fully grasp the big picture through its parts.[6]

3. EXAMINE YOUR OWN GOALS. Yet another way of finding more meaning in your work is to see how your job fits with your personal vision and purpose. Does your actual work task have relevance to your larger goals? A paycheck is meaningful to your survival, but it provides little more than support of your basic needs. If work satisfies you on a personal level, you are also more apt to see it as more meaningful.

RESILIENCE AND BELIEFS

Resiliency-boosting skills help you to make use of these three key ways of finding meaning in what you do each day. Many stressful changes and problems expose gaps in the core beliefs held by you, your coworkers, and your employer. The hardy coping and social support procedures we have presented can help you generate constructive solutions that often bridge these gaps. Resilient employees and employers call upon enduring beliefs and values to find meaning in hardship.[7]

Employees and employers sharing a common ground in beliefs increases the overall company's resilience in the face of change, as well as the resilience of the individual employees. Sharing beliefs does not mean complete agreement on everything. It is about conflict-free ways of exploring similarities and differences. The hardy attitudes of commitment, control, and challenge will provide the courage and motivation for this exploration.

What is the challenge here? If you thirst for more meaning in your work, you need to:

■ Increase your connection to the workplace and its procedures,

■ Engage more deeply in work relationships, and

■ Heighten your awareness as to the ways in which your job adds to your personal vision and purpose.

Through resiliency-boosting hardiness, you need to be open to exploring your beliefs, to see how they enhance or inhibit the problem-solving process, and to strengthen ties between you, your coworkers, and your employer. Some call this kind of challenge a "defining moment."[8]

CHRISTY'S DEFINING MOMENT

Take Christy, for example. She is a customer service supervisor for a telecommunications company. Many see her as organized, practical, reserved, and in control. She jokingly calls herself the "nursemaid of whiners," most of whom are her supervisees.

Christy dreaded going to work each day because her work task predominantly involved "putting out fires." She was tired of "codependent" supervisees who refused to do anything without her direction. Besides supervising, Christy participates in department performance reviews, and when requested, she has the "awful" job of terminating employees at her supervisor's request. It's the "messiest" part of her job, especially because of the company's "heartless" termination procedures. "I'm so tired at the end of the day, I can't muster up the energy to read or learn something new," she complained to us.

Over time, Christy's distress undermined her performance, health, and morale. The job compromised what she regarded as her core values of integrity, responsibility, citizenship, cooperation, and self-development. At first look, one might think Christy's humanistic values, talents, and skills match up nicely with customer service work tasks. If her work environment was cooperative rather than aggressive, this might be true. But, she didn't see the workplace that way at all. When Christy came to us for hardiness training, she was unenthusiastic about life, stuck in a rut, yet, to her credit, still motivated to understand this conflict

---

more clearly. The following are Christy's actual responses to our questions:

1. *What is the most stressful work conflict that is bothering you?*

"Our company is just about to undergo another round of layoffs. As part of my job, I terminate employees who are my subordinates. When there's a layoff, I end the day so fatigued that when I get home, I eat and go immediately to bed. That way, I don't have to think about it until the next day.

"I brace myself two weeks prior to company layoffs. I'm so anxious, I can think of nothing else. At these times, I feel so ineffective. Other supervisors seem to do it easily. My boss's attitude about most things is to get the job done, no matter who it hurts. What stresses me most about this situation is that some employees are laid off simply because my boss doesn't like them. She builds a case against them, and before you know it, they're gone. But, I do her dirty work. I put a lot of effort into training my supervisees. No sooner do you get to know and like them, they're let go, sometimes for frivolous reasons.

"My boss blocks department supervisors from attending management meetings. We essentially carry out her orders. But, she makes special considerations for those whom she favors.

"We have little contact with upper management. It's difficult thus to appreciate their reasons for doing things. We're in our own little world down there; it seems so pointless at times. And, the contact I do have with employees generally centers on conflicts.

"I'm bitter, pulled down, and stifled. Little is new and meaningful about my work. Because of 'bottom-line' pressures, the company regularly lets people go, and increasingly reduces employee benefits. But, the employees see the owners drive to work each day in their collection of luxury cars. And, the company just purchased a company airplane. How do I tell people I'm laying them off because the company has economic pressures? Their business practices show little integrity."

2. Is there anything about the stressful circumstance that conflicts with your core values?

"I deeply value responsibility, integrity, cooperation, citizenship, and self-development. The way my company manages layoffs really disturbs me. They're aggressive, and some of their layoff practices show little integrity and care. It's difficult enough to let someone go, but here it's a punitive rather than a supportive work environment. My boss dislikes if supervisors fraternize with supervisees, so it's difficult to know your supervisees beyond everyday work tasks. I believe it's easier to motivate people if you connect to them personally on some level. This company's policies and procedures prevent this from happening. I'm uncomfortable acting in ways counter to my social beliefs and values.

"My boss's style also really conflicts with mine. She's unpredictable, emotionally erratic, and disinterested in people. I work effectively in cooperative environments, rather than in ones in which I have to walk on eggshells."

3. Are there aspects of your work environment or relationships that fit with your core values?

"I like developing employees' professional and personal skills. To teach my supervisees constructive ways to service customers' problems—that stimulates me. Although customers can be rude at times, I feel great when I've handled them well, used the experience to teach my supervisees, and learned something new in the process myself. That's the best part of my job.

"The company also celebrates holidays, like Halloween, in a big way. Management supports personnel most during these times. Everyone participates, even the owners. We dress in costumes, and vote on the best costume of the day. The department that has the highest number of nominated employees wins an award. Everyone enjoys this event. It's healthy, cooperative competition. We get our work done, but there's lots of camaraderie. People take this event so seriously that many start to think about their costumes at the first of the year. I do what I can to make sure everyone in my area participates fully and benefits from the experience. I credit my employer for making these events important."

4. Is there a way you can bridge the gap between your own and your company's objectives and goals? Does this evaluation help you to understand more clearly the situation?

I realize more clearly now that my stress stems from a mismatch between my and the company's values and objectives. I see more clearly that I'm a fence builder rather than a fence mender. About only 30 percent of my daily work-task expresses these cooperative values. I have to find a way to balance out the costs and benefits of this job on me, or I need to look elsewhere.

"I'd involve myself more deeply in my job, if I had a clearer sense of the company's mission and goals. I'd probably cope effectively with the stressful parts of my job, if management valued employees as an economic resource. Work is more meaningful to me when the company's mission reflects social values. I know I'd get more excited about telecommunications, if my boss and employer had more of this."

CHRISTY'S INSIGHTS AND ACTIONS

Christy's stressful circumstance stemmed from perceived discrepancies between her values and the company's values. Initially, she coped regressively with this challenging stress by oversleeping and undereating. She had difficulty sorting out her thoughts and feelings about these situations, which added to her stress. For a while, Christy became anxious, depressed, and hopeless. She felt powerless, a victim of circumstance, and no longer found her work meaningful. In short, her hardy attitudes and resilience were extremely low.

As her hardiness training progressed, Christy became more insightful about herself.

First, she realized that she had not been as assisting and encouraging of her supervisees as was consistent with her humanistic values. She realized that, in her bitterness and resignation, she had begun thinking of them as "whiners," and as not being willing to take any initiative on their own.

Secondly, she had convinced herself that the company was more concerned with surviving than with thriving. Seeing her boss, and other higher management, as being uninterested in communicating with managers at her level, she had given up trying to influence them.

In other words, Christy had fallen into regressive coping with both her supervisors and supervisees, as if just holding on to her job was the most important thing, and there was no point in trying to find meaning in her work.

She began to rethink her views of the company and her role in it.

- Was the company really so comprehensively against involving the initiative of employees in developing a strategy for improving performance? After all, there was the commitment to, and preparation for, holiday parties, participated in by higher-level management as well as regular employees.

■ Was her immediate boss really so dead set against assisting and encouraging employees to do the best job they could? Although this boss terminated employees who did not seem to be doing well, she kept those that did better.

■ Were her supervisees really unwilling and unable to take any initiative in their work, or did they just feel unsupported in such efforts? After all, they showed considerable initiative and planning in the holiday celebrations the company encouraged and supported.

This line of thinking led Christy to question whether she had been, and was doing everything she could to express her values in the workplace.

■ She began to realize that she could have done more to assist and encourage proactive behavior in her supervisees.

■ It also occurred to her that she could have reached out more to her boss, expressing an understanding of the difficulties of her job, and a willingness to help by getting the department to perform better.

■ Soon, Christy was also coming up with particular plans that addressed ongoing goals and pressures, and thinking through how to communicate these possibilities not only to her supervisees, but to her immediate boss and higher management as well.

At present, it is unclear just how successful Christy will be in trying to find a closer match between her beliefs and those of her coworkers and company. But, clearly, she has gained momentum at work and at home, feeling much more energetic and directed. This hardy, resilient approach is much more likely to have a constructive effect than her previous doldrums. And if, after all else, she is unable to influence enough people in the company to feel like she belongs there, she will have the drive and self-confidence to find another job that suits her better.

SUMMARY

You are more apt to see a change as worthwhile and important to you, as worth trying to turn to advantage, and as a normal part of living, if you perceive that it expresses your values and beliefs and can deepen the meaning of what you do each day. If stressful changes undermine or poorly reflect your values, and you put little effort into trying to understand and resolve this discrepancy, you will have a difficult time being resilient. But, if you address the issues straight on and put into practice all of the coping skills and hardy attitudes we have shown you, you will at the very least be able to handle the stressful changes without being overwhelmed. In many cases, you will find that you can resolve the discrepancies through thorough examination and resilient action.

Resilience in the face of change is built on all the attributes we've discussed in this book—the hardy attitudes of commitment, control, and challenge, transformational coping skills, and developing a two-way social support system. Underlying all of this, however, is the concept of finding meaning in what you do each day. You can't expect your employer or your fellow employees to provide meaning for you. You must find it in yourself and then determine how it fits together with the company's values and those of the people with whom you work. This is the very basis of resiliency.

CHAPTER 12

HOW COMPANIES CAN BOOST RESILIENCE IN THEIR WORKERS AND IN THEMSELVES

Both companies and individuals are being forced to deal with change, not just incremental change, but dramatic, stressful change. Megatrends, such as the auspicious beginning of the information age and other dramatic technological advances, the worldwide increase in competition and redistribution of wealth, and the inexorable movement toward equal opportunity for all, have produced a rapid, indeed turbulent, rate of change that affects not only individuals and their families, but companies as well.

This book has covered the effects of stressful changes on individuals, and the things they can do to cope effectively with them. Essentially, you have to take these changes in stride and keep developing yourself, the better to turn changes to your advantage. This is why resilience is the key to your success in the modern workplace. If you are strong in the hardy attitudes, you will resiliently:

- Throw yourself into the changing circumstances (commitment) rather than back off or strike out,

- Try to identify and implement the direction implied in the changes (control) rather than throwing up your hands in defeat, and

- Consider the changes as normal and a stimulus to your development (challenge) rather than as disasters.

With the courage provided by these hardy attitudes, you will be motivated to engage in transformational coping, which is the technique and strategy for actually turning changes from potential disasters into opportunities. You will also be motivated to use the skills and strategies of social support to interact with your fellow employees in a way that builds team spirit and loyalty by giving and receiving assistance and encouragement.

Through the felicitous combination of these attitudes and skills that build resilience, you will wake up in the morning full of enthusiasm for the day, function creatively in pursuing possibilities, and feel those around you are allies in solving problems. You will not fall apart because of job changes, the need to upgrade work skills, or problematic work relationships. Instead, you will change what needs changing, accept what cannot be changed, and continue to grow and develop in the process. As time goes on, you will feel increasingly fulfilled, and your life will seem more vibrant and meaningful. You will truly be the kind of resilient person who thrives in times of change.

WHY THE OLD WAYS ARE FAILING

Overall, the more resilient employees a company or an organization has, the more successful it will be in times of change. This is because companies and organizations, like individuals, also need to be able to turn potentially disastrous changes into opportunities. The accelerating rate of economic, social, and technological change puts companies and organizations in a continual crisis mode. But, companies cannot just rely on employing more hardy, resilient individuals and hope for the best. These individuals will be increasingly uncomfortable in a company that does not have a hardy organizational quality at its core and will be likely to jump ship for some other company more suited to their proactive style and creative abilities.

In the twenty-first century, companies, like individuals, need to take seriously how they can best perform in changing times. The old, established patterns of corporate functioning seem less and less effective.

REORGANIZATIONS CAN BACKFIRE

In an effort to adapt to the pressures of our times, companies frequently downsize, merge, centralize, and decentralize in hope of competing strategically in the marketplace. Whether or not such changes bolster product lines and market presence or decrease costs to improve the bottom line, company reorganizations bring with them their own problems. Frequently, a new preoccupation with organizational changes paradoxically distracts the company from addressing the employee and customer needs that arise, and from essential tracking of marketplace developments. Trying to fill the void, new companies spring up, but they, too, often fail to address the requirements of success in a changing world.

Reorganizing companies cannot merely count on their employees and customers for loyalty and magnanimity. As individuals, many employees and customers experience the ongoing economic, technological, and social changes as threats to security and meaning. In the twenty-first century, traditional values, roles, standards, and behavior patterns beg for redefinition as society struggles to assimilate the consequences of our rapid evolution.

EMPLOYEES SEEK MEANING

The uncertainty brought by all these changes shows up in increasing employee problems of performance, conduct, morale, stamina, and health in the workplace, as well as in the home. Some examples of this are the increasing rates of divorce, workplace and school violence, civil rights and business litigation, alcohol and drug dependence, and degenerative illnesses, such as heart disease and cancer. Indeed, there is an increasing tendency for these problems to lead to lawsuits by employees against their companies for not providing effective work environments.

To their credit, companies have recently tried to improve personnel satisfaction through employee-friendly incentive programs. Examples include human resource considerations, such as bonuses, flextime, in-house babysitting, exercise facilities, and outplacement services for terminated employees. Although timely and helpful in part, such approaches fail to deal effectively with employees' dissatisfaction about having to work harder and longer, with little return in value.

With heightened social awareness and sophistication fueled by telecommunications, civil rights discussion, and widened options as the result of a strong, global economy, employees in this century require more than superficial incentives to keep them motivated, productive, and loyal to their company. Employee satisfaction polls leave no doubt that what today's workers look for and are motivated by in their jobs is a sense of purpose, continuing personal and professional development, and team effort toward a shared vision that contributes to the betterment of living.

CUSTOMER LOYALTY IS DISAPPEARING

Steadfastly insisting on good service, customers are also growing increasingly autonomous and fickle in the twenty-first century. For example, disgruntled bank consumers can now bypass the traditional banking institution altogether by operating through the Internet. So, just at the time when company reorganizations may be interfering with customized service, consumers are becoming more independent in deploying their needs. In reaching out to customers, companies have tried to offset the change-induced decrease in customized services for consumers by such means as calling their support personnel "consumer advocates," implying that customers have someone on their side in their dissatisfaction. Such approaches do little to make customers feel as if their individual needs are guiding the company's efforts and directions. If you add to this companies' increasingly detached and uncommitted workforce, you have a formula for failure.

WHAT COMPANIES NEED
TO BE RESILIENT

As you can see, current efforts on the part of most companies with regard to employees and customers are insufficient and show a misunderstanding of the problem. So, far from magnanimously granting loyalty, employees and customers are instead becoming even more distrustful and cynical concerning company aims. Thus, employees and customers are less and less inclined to make deep, lasting commitments to their companies. Today's technological and communication advances avail employees in their tendencies to bolt. Companies unable to count on their employees and customers are more likely to fail at discerning and mastering possible marketplace directions revealed by ongoing external changes, and thereby risk losing out to the competition.

What, then, is the answer for a company attempting to thrive successfully in a period of challenging economic, social, and technological transition? In brief, whether the company is undergoing a reorganization of some kind or not, it needs to become comprehensively resilient. There are two key strategies that companies use to become and remain more resilient:

1. Resilient companies develop the vision to discern changes that could undermine existing business emphases and turn them into directions of opportunity.

2. They also maintain the flexibility and strategy to act quickly in response to changes, but remain focused enough on today's needs to be competitively effective.

When these approaches have become part of a company's ingrained core culture, it is an attractive place to work for hardy individuals.

Also, these companies have a preference for selecting and training employees to be resilient in order to ensure they are proactive, innovative, enabled, and successful. Further, through the excellence of their evolving products and services, and their obvious excitement and appreciation, resilient companies are successful in convincing present and potential customers to stay with them or join them. The resilient company is continually evolving in a fashion that not only keeps it ahead of the competition in terms of products and services, but also gains and deepens the admiration and enthusiasm of its employees and clients.

CASE IN POINT: MICROSOFT

A good example of the kind of company we're talking about is Microsoft, which defined the computer software industry through its early efforts. There was so much going on, and the company's stance emphasized discerning the implicit directions in the ongoing changes of their industry and turning them into strategic efforts before anyone else could. The people in the company loved working together toward this exciting, evolving common cause.

Now, of course, concerns have mounted as to whether the

company has become monopolistic in a destructive manner. The complacency this stifling of competition might lead to, exacerbated by the enormous amount of wealth key figures in the company have made, may well undermine motivation for the proactive strategies that have been so instrumental in Microsoft's development and that of the whole industry. It's not necessarily true, however, that these pressures will actually lead to complacency.

At the present time, this resilient company and its resilient team are busy extending the scope of Internet communication into wholly different areas, such as household appliances and body parts. The time may come when not only our refrigerators, but our limbs and organs will tell us when they are no longer functioning properly, and restorative procedures will be put in place automatically. Microsoft will be a leader in such developments.

WHAT CHARACTERIZES A RESILIENT COMPANY

All companies have a culture, climate, structure, and workforce. Together, these characteristics have a pervasive, ongoing effect on the functioning and effectiveness of the organization. There is a telltale way in which these characteristics play out in resilient companies.

■ CULTURE. The values forming the culture of such companies are translations of the hardy attitudes from the individual level to the group level. Specifically, the attitudes of commitment, control, and challenge framing individual hardiness correspond at the organizational level to the hardy values of cooperation, credibility, and creativity. When individuals with hardy attitudes interact as a group, they show:

> ➤ Their attitude of commitment by valuing cooperation with each other,

> ➤ Their attitude of control by valuing that they take group responsibility for actions, and

> ➤ Their attitude of challenge by valuing creativity as they search for innovative problem solutions.

Combining into a culture, these values and attitudes provide the company with the leadership to develop products and services, while being deeply sensitive, conscientious, and caring toward employees and customers. The 3Cs of resilient values are represented prominently in the mission statement of the organization.

■ CLIMATE. The climate of a company emphasizes whether its personnel actually walk the talk of its culture. It is not enough to pay lip service to the values of the culture. They must be expressed and implemented in the ongoing interactions.

A resilient company nurtures, respects, and rewards people who employ hardy values in their day-to-day, moment-to-moment interactions with coworkers and customers. This forms a healthy environment in which people are expected to, and actually do work together in solving problems by searching for perspective and understanding and using what is learned to take decisive actions.

In interacting with each other, employees are expected to extend to others, and will want for themselves, assistance and encouragement, thereby really functioning as a team. In interacting with customers, personnel are expected to, and will maintain a deep service commitment, despite ongoing organizational, product, and market changes. When an employee exhibits the various behaviors just mentioned, the others will value it, give positive feedback, and use it as a model for their own advancement.

■ STRUCTURE. The structure of a resilient company facilitates the culture and climate described above. In most instances, a matrix management approach is used. With this approach, employees are organized into teams, each devoted to change-oriented projects, in order to facilitate rapid discernment and fulfillment of ongoing or possible directions in development of products and services.

These teams, through their team leaders, have a significant decision-making role in the organization's overall directions and emphases. All the teams in a company have available to them the advice of certain staff experts, such as industry strategists, marketers, lawyers, and accountants. Team leaders and staff experts are part of an executive committee, which functions, along with a top decision maker, to share information and consider overall company directions. Discouraged are rigidly top-down, pyramidal personnel organizations, with multiple layers of management, because they stifle flexibility, innovation, rapid response capability, and employee involvement in critical company directions.

■ WORKFORCE. To have much chance of being successful in transforming its culture, climate, and structure along resilient lines, a company has to emphasize, at the workforce level, the hardiness of its individual employees. As to personnel makeup, the resilient company must, over time, include an increasingly higher proportion of hardy individuals. This can be done through integrated use of the functions of promotions, hiring and firing, gain sharing, member benefits, and employee training to reflect the company's ongoing culture, climate, and structure.

Instrumental in these functions is the use of assessment procedures to select the resilient job applicants and training to enhance the resilience of existing employees. Despite a continually changing workplace, resilient people stay at companies high in resilience because they feel appreciated, valued, and understood. If, however, company circumstances force a crisis, hardier people leave without burning bridges behind them. They also strive proactively to find new avenues of work and maintain self-confidence.

SUMMARY

Our abiding emphasis in this book has been to show you that, at both the individual and organizational levels, there is an important choice to be made. To ensure resiliency, effectiveness, and fulfillment in our turbulent times, that choice must be to embrace the way of hardiness. This way involves developing the courage and skills that make it possible to turn stressful changes from potential disasters into opportunities.

In contrast, too many people respond bitterly and with self-pity to stressful changes. This vulnerable position is a sure formula for failure, both individually and organizationally. You must keep in mind that, however difficult the change, you choose the way you see it. Those who fall into these vulnerable ways of thinking tend to view change as imposed upon them by an impossible system. Vulnerability and failure are choices that can lead to perilous circumstances. When, instead, you find meaning in, and make good use of, stressful changes, you thrive.

NOTES

INTRODUCTION

1. J. Naisbitt, *Megatrends: Ten New Directions Transforming Our Lives* (New York: Warner Books, 1982).

CHAPTER 1:
RESILIENCE IN THE FACE OF CHANGE

1. *Quotable Quotes* (Pleasantville, New York: Reader's Digest, 1977) p. 166.

2. G. Schule, *Stress at the Naked Edge*, Videotape. (Irvine, Calif.: Jerdan Productions, 2004).

CHAPTER 2:
RESEARCHING STRESS AND RESILIENCY

1. R. King, *Michelangelo and the Pope's Ceiling* (New York: Walker & Company, 2003), pp. 1–304.

2. S. R. Maddi and S. C. Kobasa, *The Hardy Executive: Health Under Stress* (Homewood, Ill.: Dow Jones-Irwin, 1984).

CHAPTER 3:
HOW HARDINESS PROMOTES RESILIENCE

1. W. B. Cannon, *Bodily Changes in Pain, Hunger, Fear, and Rage*, 2nd ed. (New York: Appleton, 1929).

2. P. T. Bartone, "Hardiness Protects Against War-Related Stress in Army Reserve Forces," *Consulting Psychology Journal*, 1999, 51, pp. 72–82.

3. P. T. Bartone, R. J. Ursano, K. M. Wright, and L. H. Ingrahm, "The Impact of a Military Air Disaster on the Health of Assistance Workers: A Prospective Study," *Journal of Nervous and Mental Disease*, 1989, 177, pp. 317–328.

4. K. D. Allred and T. W. Smith, "The Hardy Personality: Cognitive and Physiological Responses to Evaluative Threat," *Journal of Personality and Social Psychology*, 1989, 56, pp. 257–266.

5. K. Lancer, "Hardiness and Olympic Women's Synchronized Swim Team" (presentation given at University of Nevada, Las Vegas, 2000).

6. S. R. Maddi and M. Hess, "Personality Hardiness and Success in Basketball," *International Journal of Sports Psychology*, 1992, 23, pp. 360–368.

7. P. T. Bartone and S. A. Snook, "Cognitive and Personality Factors Predict Leader Development in U.S. Army Cadets" (paper presented at 35th International Applied Military Psychology Symposium (IAMPS), Florence, Italy, May 1999).

8. M. Westman, "The Moderating Effect of Hardiness on the Relationship Between Stress and Performance," *Human Performance*, 1990, 3, pp. 141–155.

9. D. Lifton, S. Seay, and A. Bushke, "Can Student Hardiness Serve as an Indicator of Likely Persistence to Graduation? Baseline Results from a Longitudinal Study," *Academic Exchange Quarterly*, Winter, 2000, pp. 73–81.

10. S. R. Maddi, P. Wadhwa, and R. J. Haier, "Relationship of Hardiness to Alcohol and Drug Use in Adolescents," *American Journal of Drug and Alcohol Abuse,* 1996, 22, pp. 247–257.

11. E. W. McCranie, V. A. Lambert, and C.E. Lambert, "Work Stress, Hardiness, and Burnout Among Hospital Staff Nurses," *Nursing Research*, 1987, 36, pp. 374–378.

12. C. Giatris, "Personality Hardiness: A Predictor of Occupational Stress and Job Satisfaction Among California Fire Service Personnel" (master's thesis, California State University, Long Beach, 2000).

13. M. Atella, "Crossing Boundaries: Effectiveness and Health Among Western Managers Living in China," *Consulting Psychology Journal*, 1999, 51, pp. 125–134.

14. S. R. Maddi and D. M. Khoshaba, *HardiSurvey III-R: Test Development and Internet Instruction Manual* (Newport Beach, Calif.: Hardiness Institute, 2001).

CHAPTER 4:

YOU CAN *LEARN* TO BE RESILIENT

1. D. M. Khoshaba and S. R. Maddi, "Early Antecedents of Hardiness," *Consulting Psychology Journal*, 1999, 51, pp. 106–116.

2. F. Rhodewalt and J. B. Zone, "Appraisal of Life Change, Depression, and Illness in Hardy and Nonhardy Women," *Journal of Personality and Social Psychology*, 1989, 56, pp. 81–88.

3. D. M. Khoshaba and S. R. Maddi, *HardiTraining* (Newport Beach, Calif.: Hardiness Institute, 2004).

4. S. R. Maddi, "Hardiness Training at Illinois Bell Telephone," in *Health Promotion Evaluation*, J. P. Opatz, ed. (Stevens Point, Wis.: National Wellness Institute, 1987), pp. 101–115.

5. P. T. Bartone, R. J. Ursano, K. M. Wright, and L. H. Ingraham, "The Impact of a Military Air Disaster on the Health of Assistance Workers: A Prospective Study," *Journal of Nervous and Mental Disease*, 1989, 177, pp. 317–328; R. J. Contrada, "Type A Behavior, Personality Hardiness, and Cardiovascular Responses to Stress," *Journal of Personality and Social Psychology*, 1989, Vol. 57, No.5, pp. 895–903.

6. S. R. Maddi, D. M. Khoshaba, K. Jensen, E. Carter, J. Lu, and R. Harvey, "Hardiness Training for High-Risk Undergraduates," *NACADA Journal*, 2002, 22, pp. 45–55.

CHAPTER 5:

DO YOU HAVE THE RIGHT ATTITUDES TO THRIVE IN ADVERSITY?

1. J. Cook, comp., *The Book of Positive Quotations* (New York: Gramercy Books, 1999), p. 256.

2. A. S. Mak and J. Mueller, "Job Insecurity, Coping Resources, and Personality Dispositions in Occupational Strain," *Work & Stress*, 2000, Vol. 14, No. 4, pp. 312–328.

3. T. Tarthang, "Skillful Means," in *Mindfulness and Meaningful Work: Explorations in Right Livelihood*, C. Whitmyer, ed. (Berkeley, Calif.: Parallax Press, 1994), pp. 28–31.

4. J. Cook, comp., *The Book of Positive Quotations* (New York: Gramercy Books, 1999), p. 520.

5. J. Cook, comp., *The Book of Positive Quotations* (New York: Gramercy Books, 1999), p. 502.

CHAPTER 7:
TRANSFORMATIONAL COPING: TURNING STRESSFUL CHANGES TO YOUR ADVANTAGE

1. W. Dyer, *There's a Spiritual Solution to Every Problem* (New York: HarperCollins, 2001), p. 40.

2. A. Cohen, *I Had It All the Time: When Self-Improvement Gives Way to Ecstasy* (Haiku, Hawaii: Alan Cohen Publications, 1994), p. 145.

3. J. Cook, comp., *The Book of Positive Quotations* (New York: Gramercy Books, 1999), p. 502.

4. J. Cook, comp., *The Book of Positive Quotations* (New York: Gramercy Books, 1999), p. 517.

CHAPTER 9:
SOCIAL SUPPORT: GIVING AND RECEIVING ASSISTANCE AND ENCOURAGEMENT

1. S. D. Rushnell, *When God Winks: How the Power of Coincidence Guides Your Life* (Hillsboro, Ore.: Beyond Words Publishing, 2001), p. 145.

2. W. H. Kuo and Y. Tsai, "Social Networking, Hardiness, and Immigrants' Mental Health," *Journal of Health and Social Behavior*, 1986, Vol. 27, No.2, pp. 133–149.

CHAPTER 10:
PRACTICING SOCIALLY SUPPORTIVE INTERACTIONS

1. D. L. Turnipseed, "Hardy Personality: A Potential Link with Organizational Citizenship Behavior," *Psychological Reports*, October 2003, Vol. 93, Issue 2, pp. 529–544.

CHAPTER 11:
STRENGTHENING EMPLOYEE AND EMPLOYER TIES

1. M. W. Edelman, *The Measure of Our Success: Letter to My Children and Yours*. (New York: Perennial Currents, 1993), p. 40.

2. "What Your Disaffected Workers Cost," *The Gallup Management Journal*, 2001, pp. 12–20.

3. "What Your Disaffected Workers Cost," *The Gallup Management Journal*, 2001, pp. 12–20; S. Crabtree, "Beyond the Dot-Com Bust." *The Gallup Management Journal*, December 11, 2003, 3, pp. 42–56.

4. S. R. Maddi, "The Search for Meaning," in M. Page, ed., *Nebraska Symposium on Motivation* (Lincoln, Neb.: University of Nebraska Press, 1970), 18, pp. 137–185; S. R. Maddi, "The Existential Neurosis," *Journal of Abnormal Psychology*, 1970, Vol. 72, No. 3, pp. 11–325.

5. T. W. Britt, A. B. Adler, and P. T. Bartone, "Deriving Benefits from Stressful Events: The Role of Engagement in Meaningful Work and Hardiness," *Journal of Occupational Health Psychology*, January 2001, Vol. 6, No. 1, pp. 53–63.

6. J. Isaksen, "Constructing Meaning Despite the Drudgery of Repetitive Work." *Journal of Humanistic Psychology*, July 1, 2000, Vol. 40, No. 3, pp. 84–107.

7. D. L. Coutu, "How Resilience Works," *Harvard Business Review*, May 1, 2002, pp. 2–7.

8. J. L. Badaracco, "The Discipline of Building Character," *Harvard Business Review*, March 1, 1998.

INDEX

and case studies of people low in resilience, 74–80
by expressing resiliency skills, 82–84
by studying highly resilient people,
65–67
by turning stress to your advantage,
72–73
practicing socially supportive interactions, 155–177
by building pattern of encourage-
ment/assistance, 166–170
by communicating constructively,
165–166
by creating social interaction map,
157–160
by implementing/evaluating action
plan, 170–176
by solving conflicts with assistance/
encouragement, 160–170
practicing transformational coping,
107–133
and continuation of transformational
coping process, 132–133
by creating/implementing action
plan, 124–132
by finding alternatives, 110–113
by identifying unresolved stressful
circumstances, 108–110
by searching for perspective/under-
standing, 113–116
by Situational Reconstruction,
110–124
and Situational Reconstruction case
studies, 119–124
by understanding stressors, 116–119
purpose, sense of, 40, 41
pyramidal organizations, 199

Ratzenberger, John, 55
reflection, feedback from, 128
regressive coping
case studies of, 93–104
self-assessment for, 105
transformational coping vs., 92–93
relationships
for social support, 138–139

supportive interactions to improve,
45
transformational coping with, 87–88
at work, 181
see also practicing socially supportive
interactions
reorganization of companies, 193–194
research
on hardiness, 31–37
on resilience, 15–26, *see also* resilience research
on stress, 15–17
resilience, 2–3
in companies, *see* company resiliency
boosters
early experiences undermining,
41–42
and hardiness, 3–4, 13–14
at home, 22
influence of attitudes on, 54–61, *see
also* attitude(s) for resilience
key to, 3–4, 13–14
power of, 12–13
roots of, 17–19
resilience research, 15–26
Illinois Bell Telephone project, 16–17
nonresilient manager case study
from, 24–25
resilient manager case study from,
20–23
and roots of resilience, 17–19
and vulnerability, 23–24
resiliency skills, 82–84, 182–183
resilient managers, 20–23
resources, sharing, 139, 167
responsibility(-ies)
assistance with, 139, 167
for stress, 69
results, feedback from, 128
rigidity, 56

sabotage, 93
self-assessment
for attitudes for resilience, 61–63
for regressive coping, 105
for social support, 152–153